JULY 4 - '06

In Care of Yellow River

Eli Pinson Landers

In Care of
Yellow River

The Complete Civil War Letters of
Pvt. Eli Pinson Landers
to His Mother

ELIZABETH WHITLEY ROBERSON

Drawings by
Stephen McCall

PELICAN PUBLISHING COMPANY
Gretna 1997

First published by Venture Press in Fort Lauderdale, Florida, 1994
Published by arrangement with the author

First Pelican edition, 1997

The word "Pelican" and the depiction of a pelican are trademarks
of Pelican Publishing Company, Inc., and are registered
in the U.S. Patent and Trademark Office.

Library of Congress Cataloging-in-Publication Data

Landers, Eli Pinson.
    In care of Yellow River : the complete Civil War letters of Pvt.
Eli Pinson Landers to his mother / Elizabeth Whitley Roberson ;
drawings by Stephen McCall. — 1st Pelican ed.
      p.   cm.
    Originally published: Fort Lauderdale, Fla. : Venture Press, 1994.
    Includes index.
    ISBN 1-56554-245-2 (pbk. : alk. paper)
    1. Landers, Eli Pinson—Correspondence. 2. United States—
History—Civil War, 1861-1865—Personal narratives, Confederate.
3. Confederate States of America. Army. Georgia Infantry Regiment,
16th—Biography. 4. Georgia—History—Civil War, 1861-1865—
Personal narratives. 5. Soldiers—Georgia—Gwinnett County—
Correspondence. 6. Gwinnett County (Ga.)—Biography.
I. Roberson, Elizabeth Whitley. II. Title.
E503.5 16th.L36 1997
973.7'458'092—dc21
[B]   96-37989
                                              CIP

Manufactured in the United States of America

Published by Pelican Publishing Company, Inc.
1101 Monroe Street, Gretna, Louisiana 70053

This book is dedicated to the memory of
Eli Pinson Landers and to his comrades in
arms of the 16th Regiment, Georgia
Volunteers, Flint Hill Grays, who gave
their very lives for the right to live in a free
and independent nation.

-EWR

Other Books
by Elizabeth Whitley Roberson

Weep Not for Me, Dear Mother

Contents

Foreword

The letters contained in this book were thrown away in the 1960's on a street in Atlanta for the trash man to dispose of. Luckily, they were retrieved by an interested passer-by and after twenty years, fell into my possession. After reading them in chronological order, I realized how valuable these letters were and decided to write of the battles in which Eli participated by using his letters to give them a more personal flavor. It was that narrative that I published in Weep Not for Me, Dear Mother.

In many instances, I simply pulled the most descriptive passages from the letters, which meant that I had to leave out many small details, which in retrospect were very important. I now realize that every word he wrote had meaning for someone. For that reason I have compiled all of Eli Landers' letters, including the fragments, here in the order in which they were written, beginning with the very first one he wrote, on August 11, 1861, the morning he left home, to the letter he wrote on October 2, 1863, two weeks before he died in a hospital in Rome, Georgia.

In making the decision as to where the original letters should be put, I felt that Eli would have wanted them to "go back home", so with the permission of Mrs. Nellie Mobley, who had loaned them to me, I gave them to the Gwinnett County Historical Society in Lawrenceville, Georgia, in whose possession they rest today.

Family Background

The Landers family story originally begins in England, but by the early 1700's the Landers had emigrated to the colony of Virginia. One of the first Landers to come to America was Luke Landers of Hanover County, Virginia. His son, Tyree Landers, was born in Virginia in 1760 and served in the American Revolution. In 1784, he married Francis Davis, the daughter of Humphrey Davis, in Wake County, North Carolina. In 1790, they moved to Elbert County, Georgia with their four sons. In 1814, one of the sons, Humphrey Davis Landers, married Sarah Brawner.

In 1820, a land lottery was held for families who wanted to move to new undeveloped sections of Georgia. The names of the families were put in a box and as each name was called, a slip of paper with the lot and district written on it was drawn from the box and given to the person who drew it out. Humphrey Davis Landers drew lot No. 177 in the 6th Land District in Gwinnett County, the area now called Lilburn.

He and his wife and four children then moved south to claim their land. During the next few years, four more children were born but in 1831, his wife died. Two of the eight children had died in infancy. Left with six children, ranging in ages from one year to sixteen years of age, Humphrey married again very soon after his wife's death. He married young Susan McDaniel, who over the next few years gave him eight more children, one of whom was Eli Pinson Landers.

Eli was raised in a family that fostered a deep spiritual faith. His grandfather, Tyree, was a Baptist minister who was responsible for the founding of at least three Primitive Baptist churches in the county. In 1824, he gave two acres of land for the Sweetwater Church. Eli's family belonged to this church and he mentions it quite frequently in his letters. The religious training he received there provided him with a "coat of armor" that helped him accept the terrible conditions in which he found himself as the war dragged on and to believe that no matter what happened to him, it was God's will.

One only has to read a few of Eli's letters to marvel at the proficiency with which he wrote. The ability to write this well was not true of the average young man of the 1860's but Eli's family tradition of a love of learning gave him this ability to express his thoughts so eloquently. Before the Sweetwater Church was built, records indicate that their services were held in the Wells Schoolhouse, so apparently it was here that Eli received his formal education. It could also have been in the Center Academy, incorporated in 1839, in which his father served as trustee.

Eli's father died when Eli was quite young, and he and his brothers and sisters helped their mother tend the farm on which they grew wheat and corn. By the time of the outbreak of the War Between the States however, all of the children were married and living in their own homes, except Eli and his younger sister, Caroline. It appears that the other brothers and sisters lived close by and did assist their mother in the plowing and planting.

Soon after the battle of First Manassas, Howell Cobb of Athens, Georgia organized a regiment of men in and around Gwinnett County. It was called the 16th Regiment of Georgia Volunteers and was composed of ten companies A through J. Eli joined Co. H, which was known as the "Flint Hill Grays." His company was mustered in on August 11, 1861, and they left immediately by train from Stone Mountain for Richmond, Virginia. They were stationed in and around the Richmond area for several months. Eli was taken

12

sick a few weeks after his arrival there and stayed in a private home for over six weeks. He was allowed to go home on sick leave in December, 1861, the only time he was ever able to visit his family before his death in 1863.

Upon his return to duty in January, 1862, he joined his unit near Yorktown. In April, his regiment engaged in their first serious battle with Federal forces at Dam No. I on the Warwick River. From there they moved back toward Richmond, where they were involved in the Seven Days Battle. Their next major engagement was at the Battle of Crampton's Gap at South Mountain, Maryland. It was there that over two thirds of the 16th Regiment was killed or captured by the enemy. A few months later, they were involved in the battles of Fredericksburg and Chancellorsville. In July of 1863, they marched into Pennsylvania with the Army of Northern Virginia and participated in the Battle of Gettysburg.

Soon after their return to Virginia, they joined forces with Longstreet's Division, which had been called to Chattanooga to help defend Georgia from invasion by Federal troops. They arrived in Georgia in September, in time for the battle of Chickamauga, which Eli survived, only to die a few weeks later of typhoid fever!

These letters describe quite graphically the battles in which the 16th was engaged and gives us a vivid picture of camp life in the 1860's. Nearly lost to posterity, these letters survive here as a tribute to the young man who so willingly gave his life for the cause of the Confederacy.

Family References in Landers Letters

In order to understand the relationship of the members of Eli's family, it is necessary to know their names, as well as their nicknames, which were often used throughout the letters. They are as follows:

SISTERS:
(1) Hildy Caroline Landers - "H.C." or "Car"- unmarried

(2) Rebecca Adaline Landers - "R.A." or "Add" married to Morten Hutchins– "Moten"–died July,1862 child, William Henry ("Little W.H.") died November,1862

(3) Elizabeth Landers ("Liz") married Willard Pinckney Mason ("W.P." or "Pink") who was killed November 27,1862. Children- Charles and Maryanne married second time - Sam Dyer

(4) Harriet Landers married to Daniel Minor - died November 6, 1863 child- Eli Pinson - "Little Eel"

BROTHERS:
(1) Napoleon Bonaparte Landers-"N.B." or "Pole" (died at Vicksburg July 26,1863) married Sarah McGinnis child-"Little Pole"

(2) Humphrey Davis Landers-"H.D." married Wealthy Fowler child-Humphrey Davis III -"Little H.D." Joined Co. G., 30th Alabama Infantry. Captured May 16, 1863 at Champion Hill, Missisippi. Paroled July 4th, 1863 and recaptured at Nashville, Tennessee Dec. 16th, 1864.

COUSINS:
(1) Elijah Moore McDaniel- "E.M." or "Lige" captured at Cold Harbor, Va. June 1,1864. Released from Elmira, N.Y. on June 16,1865

(2) Archibald Washington McDaniel- "A.W." or "Arch"

Uncle Ely and Aunt Cebell - His mother, Susan's brother and wife, the parents of Elijah and Archibald.

1861

August 11, 1861

This is the 11th day of the month and I must write some more to let you no that the time has come close to hand when I must close the old cottage door. They are now getting breakfast and when I eat I will start to the Stone Mountain to leave there at half past 9 o'clock tonight. If nothing happens I will eat my breakfast in Augusta in the morning and I will mail this letter today at the Mountain. But we have a fine set of boys going. All are our settlement Boys but Bill Miner. Tell Barry Brasell that he has missed the best chance in the world. My hand and heart trembles so this morning that I cant rite much as I would for the thoughts of leaving Gwinnett and my Mamma and friends in general. I have said nothing about domestic business in my letter nor dont expect to. My time is short here. Breakfast is nearly ready and then I must start. But if I never see you again take care of yourself and I will try to do the same. So no more only truly remains your affectionate Brother until Death.

E.P. Landers to H.D. Landers

Richmond, Va
August the 15th , 1861
Dear Mother,

I have got a small chance to drop you a few lines to let you know that I have landed at Richmond yesterday evening and are well as common and tolerable well satisfied but very much wearied and tired. I am now 7 hundred miles from you all. We ate breakfast in Augusta Monday morning. We got there about sun rise. The citizens of Augusta give us our breakfast and treated us well. There was a young lady give me a flag made of silk ribbon and told me to take it to Va but some grand raskal stold it. The people both men and ladies give us the praise all the way. They hurahed for Georgia for she carrys the day here at Conier's Station. The tracks was full of ladies and fellas. I fell in love with one of them. She had on a dress like Adds white one. Mamma, I came all through old S.C. and the woods are not all cleared up yet. I have seed a heap of sites since I left home more than I could write in a week and I went in a heap of dangers. I traveled over a bridge about 25 to 40 feet high which was about 3 miles long. On Monday night we got to Wilmington about midnight. There we changed cars. There was a large river run through that town which we had to cross in a steamboat as big as our lot. The river was about one and a half miles wide. Then the next place was Petersburg. We stayed at night there in a house made a purpose for soldiers. Atlanta is a baby to this town. It is 22 miles from Richmond. Richmond is a great place. I have seed more people since I left home. Tell William Henry I want to see him so bad. I can look back and can just see my old home and everything about it but I don't know whether I ever will see it again or not. We think that we will be ordered to Manassas Junction in about 3 weeks. We are camped on Old Scotts Land but he is afraid to come on it. There has been another fight in Missouri. We whipt them thunder. I can set here and look out yonder in the field and see 1000 men drilling one squad, so I must quit again. Write soon. I would like to see you very bad specially you Mamma. Tell the girls to write. I would like to hear from them so I have to send you this letter but I can't come with it so no more at present only truly remaining your affectionate son until Death.

Farewell to Susan Landers.

August 15, 1861
Dear Mother,

There are about 13000 men campt at this place. I walked out on the field yesterday evening and saw Col.Sim's [Semme's] Regiment drill. It was the prettiest sight I ever saw. We was mustered in survice this morning. They all looked very serious. We put up our tents yesterday evening and this morning took them down again to move one mile but I reckon we won't go. There are so many folks around me that I can't write. There are hundreds of men out before me drilling. I have saw a heep of my old friends. I saw Burd Martin. He has got about well. He will go back to his company next week. Our tents looks like a little town. I reckon there are a thousand tents here. We and Thomases Company met a grinning like possums. Bob Elis met us a half mile from camp. I can't write much but I could tell you a heep if I could see you. We got plenty to eat meat and bread and rice and sugar and coffey. We can write what we please. Tell Moten and Pole they don't no nothing. I left them on Sunday night and I reckon I got away from them fast enough. Mamma and Car you may find me some good clothes for this is cold here of a morning. I have got on both of my coats and am not too warm. Tell the girls not to forget me and I want them to write to me and tell Paulina that the left side of my coat is not ript yet. There are one regiment now leaving here to go to Fare Creek. The artillery is now saluting them by firing cannons. They have fired 5 times. I saw the artillery yesterday evening with their guns and cannons. I saw ten cannons in Kinston which was about 10 feet long. Give my love to all my friends and girls. W.P.

Mason is well, only he has got something in his eye. He said to tell Liz he won't write this time. It is no use. He will write before long. Tell Bill Miner that he will miss all the fun if he don't come. Mamma if you can, send me a flannel pair of drawers and a camp cap. Bill Dyer is as big a fool as ever. He is now plaguing a man. There are a heep of calls for money here but I han't spent but 5 cts yet only what I spent on the way here. You can't hear nothing but drums and fifes here hardly. They have got lots of prisoners in Richmond. I am going back in town to see them today. I have not forgot the advice Mamma but there is a heep temptations here. I could write more but it is so confused. Take care of yourselfs and write soon. Direct your letters to Richmond, Va Howell Cobb's Regiment in care of Captain Richardson and it will come rite here. Tell So Turner that we have got away from our families at last! So now I must quit.

Your son, E P Landers

Richmond
August 18, 1861
Dear Mother and Brothers and Sisters,

This Monday morning after coming back from drilling I am much wearied. I seat myself to tell you that I am in my tent by myself and to tell you that I am well this morning. I promised you that I would write you the truth if I could but it is impossible to do it although I am allowed to write what I please. When I wrote you the first letter I had just got here and had not seed much then but my eyes has been opened since then. We moved from that campground the next morning after we got here to about one mile to the old fair grounds. There is about 5 acres in it. They keep guard out all the time and we cant pass out nor in without taking a pass from the Captain. It is hard for a white man to tote a written pass like a Negro! The Gwinnett Negroes is free to the side of us but don't tell Bill Miner. Let him come. There is two just come out of the guard house. They was put in night before last. I met up with twenty two hundred of my enemies yesterday evening but they was prisoners. They was stout looking fellers. Tell the people to quit talking about Little Yankeys for they are Big Devils and do look so mean that I could not help from cussing them! I just shook my fist at them and they did look at us so mean. I saw them come out to go to get water. Some was barefooted and some without a shirt. There was one man stood off and curst them of the meanest devils that he could think of.

I wrote to you that it was cold here and it was then in the morning but it is as hoter day today as I ever experienced. The sweat is now running down my cheeks. We have had enough to eat till last night. We did not have a bite of bread for supper only what we bought because the quartermaster drawed rations for 5 days and it give out.

I got permission from my captain and went up in town today. There I saw the greatest place I ever did see! Atlanta is nothing more than a kitchen to the Big house! I will tell you folks that there is no use in trying to compare nothing to what I have saw since I left home! I saw Washington's Monument. It is away up on a stack of fine rock and he is on the largest horse that I ever saw. Washington is on that horse with his sword in his hand. The horse and man looks as natural as nature itself. Just get out of the way because it looks just like its coming right onto you! It is larger than any man or horse you ever saw. And I shook hands with old Zachary Taylor yesterday evening. He looks just as natural as the man itself. It is about the size of a man. Its made of tombstone. You can see the coat buttons and neck ties even down to his shoe strings. Well I cant tell you as plain as it is.

We are a long ways apart and we are 750 miles apart and I am here trying to tell conditions. We expect to be called tomorrow as soon as we get drilled enough but we are ready to start anytime. They had a fight in Missouri on the 16th. We killed and wounded 3 or 4 thousand and was still in pursuit of them with a large body of cavalry and was likely to destroy all of them which I am in hopes they will. They had a fight in 32 miles of us on Wednesday night. The Yankeys killed and wounded 500 of our men but we whipt them in the Fight. We don't know how many we killed of them but they drove 1400 of those Yankeys up in Richmond to take supper with us. This is the report.

Mamma I want to see you and Car the worst you ever saw! Its not been long since I saw you but it seems like it has been a month but don't you study about me for if I am called to the field I hope that I will come out unhurt but if I never see old Gwinnett let my post stand. Tell Miss Cody that I was glad I have got out of her cotton patch!

There is some of our boys sick but not bad. I would like to see some of the old Gwinnett peach peelings and watermelon rinds. We hardly ever get anything of that kind but we must make out without them. We are here in this place and cant get out. We are like birds in a cage. But Mother dont let none of this trouble you for I tam just reconciled to my lot. I have give myself up to Providence and I hope that I will be present both soul and body. Give my best respects and love to all the connections and friends. The drum has beat and I must get in line or else be imprisoned 24 hours in the guardhouse. Thom Sanders was absent the other night and he was kept in the gurad house a night and a day.

We have got back from drilling and it is raining. I will try to finish this letter. We all done very well in the drill. I want you to write to me as often as you can and pay the postage of your letter if you can and write the news in

21

general. You know what I want to hear. Tell all the people to write that will but it is a bad chance for me to write. Tell the girls to write for I would like to hear from all my old friends. Write how the crops look and if it has rained any there or not. We have plenty rain here. It has been half shoe mouth deep round our tent but it is drying up. But there is a likely prospect for more rain. Tell W.T. Mathews to come on with Cain if he wants to see Yankeys for they are no sight of them here. Tell him to to write. Tell Bill Carel to write and for Pillard. Tell Moten and Pole I have not forgot how they stood round the car by me but I rolled from them fast. Tell them to write to me. W.P. Mason is complaining with his back. He never went on drill this evening. Tell the folks to not wait for me to write to them. Mamma I have always tried to take care of you but now you must take care of yourself. We have to buy our bread for supper or eat beef and rice. Write soon. Tell Mrs. Sintha Boles that I saw her Mack. I thought of her when I saw the lady. It made me think of my old settlement. Give my respects to all the girls in the settlement and the old women too. Tell them to write some more. This letter closes with thoughts in Gwinnett. Truly remaining your affectionate son and brother till death.

E.P. Landers to all the Family

Richmond, Va
August the 29th 1861
Dear Mother,

This morning I take pleasure in writing to you. These lines leave me well hoping that these lines will reach you. Well I have written 3 or 4 letters back home and have never received a line from none of you yet but I will write to you even if I never hear from you. I will make you pay the postage for the chance is bad for me to get money for it is all the consolation I have is to think of my friends in Gwinnett. But I am in a crowd of friends here.

I have just bin up in town to see Joe Waldrop. He has come from Manasses here with the rheumatism. He is staying at a private home and is treated like a child. I visit him every day. Tell old [?] I saw some of her hair here in Richmond! Joe had it braided. He was in that battle at Manasses but never got hurt only one bullet went through his hat and lightly scalped his head. He is a Methodist preacher and is with his old brethren. He is the same old Joe. We enjoyed ourselves well together and he was so proud to see us. I heard of him and started right out to hunt for him and I found him in a grocery store and nothing would do him but I must drink with him. Him and Bill Carel is in the same house. Bill Cotheren is in the same house too. There is 100 sick in our regiment but none fatal. Our officers is all sick, that is the the Commissioned officers all but Luit Smith and it keeps him all his time to keep things straightened out. Our Capt.is now in town in a private house. I fear that he will not stand it long though.

We may not have to say here long. We expect to leave here soon to go to Savannah, Georgia but I don't much want to go there but we will leave here before long. If times don't get worse than they are now I expect to come home sometime this winter.I can get a furlow for 30 days if the times are not exciting. Joe says when he gets well enough to travel he is going home. He talks like coming by my old Sacred home.

It is raining here today. The mud is half shoe mouth deep but we all take it finely though it is not like it is at home on wet days. We get plenty to eat and there is 22 of us has throde in and hired a Negro man to cook for us. It cost us 17 and a half cents a week! He is a good cook.

We got a letter from Manasses the other day. John Matthews and George Mills, Nicholas Shamblee, and George Garner, T.P.Hudson was sick with the mumps and measels. The mumps and measels are in our camp but I have not took them yet. I have been pestered with my throat ever since we been here but I am looking every day when I will take some disease for it is so disagreeable here. Tell the Gwinnett folks that I have not forgotten their respects give me while I was there. It is anomating to think of the way the people done at the Mountain that night we started. It was bad to part with friends but God bless them is my prayer if I never see them again. Give my best love to all the connections excepting none. Tell Miss Lizabeth Carrel that I wish her much joy and great success in the remaining part of life. Tell her that the morning I started I had rather a saw her than any other one on earth and have been sorrored ever since and since I heard of the wedding even more so. Tell Miss Paulina Couch that the left side of my coat has not ripped yet.

Send my love up in my old settlement if I can't carry it there myself. This old war is opened up at last and thank God for it! It will be Death or Victory but if to the latter I want them either to fight it out or quit one. So help me pray for a fight or peace. We see bad times here. The guard is now out in the rain. I was out the other night in the hardest rain and wind. We have Yankeys here no end to them and I have saw them till I don't like to look at them. If they take many more we will stay here to guard them.

Bill DeShong is now playing the fiddle. It makes me think of my old settlement almost with tears in my eyes. I want you to write Mamma and write long letters like me. Write like you was talking to me. Write how things stands about home and how my filly is getting on. Take good care of her for she is all I have got. Tell Moten to break the little steers for it may be that I will be with him and if I don't tell him to not forget me nor to write. Mamma if you please make me some good warm winter clothes against winter time but keep them till I send for them. I may not be here but you can get the settlememt to join in and box them up and send them by express.

I have just eat my dinner. We had beef dumplings and bread but I would like to have some of your buttermilk and bread and peaches to eat after I get done. Tell N.B. to stay at home for he can't stand it but a little while in such weather as this for there is now about 8 or 10 of our boys sick. We don't muster but about 60 men. Mamma the reason I write so often is becauise it is through repects. Tell all Uncle Ely's folks that Lige and Arch is well and as well satisfied as I am. We got their letter yesterday and it was gratifying to me to hear from you and to hear that you all was in good spirits. That is the way to be. But be humble. Don't boast.

I wish that I could be with you this evening. I could tell you more than a little but it may be that my presence will never be in your yard anymore. Tell James Garner that his blanket has done me more good than a little but tell Charles McInnis to keep his durned old blanket! Give my respects to all and tell Aunt Polly's folks to write soon. Play with William Henry and Pole and Charles for me. So goodby to you all. This may be the last letter from Richmond if we have to leave so no more at present only I remain your affectionate son till Death. Write soon.

To Susan Landers from E.P. Landers

Richmond, Va
September the 5th 1861
Dear Mother and Friends,

I take pleasure in returning compliments for such a kind letter as I received this morning from you all. It found me well and hearty. I was glad to hear from you. It gives me pleasure for my friends to be kind to send their respects to me. It checks my feelings so to read a letter from any of you that I can't keep from crying to save my life. I cried hearty when I read my Mother's few lines that she wrote. You want me to write the truth but I can only write what I see to be the truth for we can't hear it. Times is bad here and getting worse. There is so much sickness here. There is about 250 sick in this regiment. They are dying dayly. There has been about 15 died since last Sunday morning. Last Thursday there was 6 died. Two died in about fifteen minutes between their deaths though I have not bin sick but one day since I left home. The sick is just lying thick through the camps on a little straw with their knapsacks under their heads or something else. It's like Brutus to see a man die in such places but they can't help theirself for Col. Cobb wont allow them to be moved out of camp if he can help it but the most of them gets their friends to go out and get a house for them and then we steal them off to the house. Five or six of our sick ones run away the other evening and went to private houses. We have 42 sick in our company. We are badly wearied waiting on them. Cousin Jo is down with his pains yet. He is at the same place. He can't write but sends his compliments to you all. He has not heard from his folks lately. He wrote to them the other day. W.T. Smith is in the same house with the measels. You write that you wanted to see me so bad but you are in as greater confusion as I am. You would like to see anybody but Howell Cobb. It would gratify my soul and body just to see you all again. I can just see you all and the old place just as plain as daylight in my imagination. Tell all the girls howdy for me and tell them to write to me for I have not the chance to write much and tell Jane Shamblee that I saw a letter start to her yesterday from "Underlip". Tell Rachel to write to me and write the fun. Car what was it that made Jane cry so? I have forgot. Tell her that I said God bless her and may the Devil miss her! Tell her I'll see her again. Give my sincere and best love to all that mentions my name in charity. You wrote that you had help to save your fodder. I want to know how you will get it. Be sure and give my best thanks to all that pretends to help Mother and Car for I never will forget them for it. I want you all to be charitable and live in peace for there is no peace here though we enjoy ourselves as well as we can. That lady that I was telling you about still says she will attend to me if I get sick. Their names is Hix. They grumble at me if I don't go out to see them everyday. They say that I am just like their brother that is in the same cause I am. She says she is coming to Georgia with me when I come home but if they don't come till I do it will be a good while before they come for there is no prospect that I can see if times don't get better. I want you to take care of my mare for I want to take some good long rides when I get home. I want to go to see Jane and Emily. You wanted to know who I was mest with. It's me and Lige and Arch, Dave Cruse, Bob, Jim and Ben, Thom Matthews and Trainum. Me, Lige, Arch, Dave, and Trainum sleep together. We have only got 4 blankets in our tent but we do tolerable well as the weather is yet tolerable warm but when winter comes we will need more cover. There is some ladies in our company now with some nourishments for the sick. They are deeply interested. They think a heap of the Georgia Boys! I will send this letter by Charles Making if I can get it written before he starts. Tell William Henry to keep out of the fire or he'll get burnt bad sometime. Tell him he need not to look for me so don't fool the little fellow no more. Tell all the little grandchildren howda for me and tell Harriet that we can't get to the Yankeys to whip them and I don't know when I will get home and as for the other word she sent, it is good if I could only perform the work but there is so many temptations to lead me away. It is a place of wickedness. You wanted to know if we had anything to put in our bread. We have salt though we buy soda to put in it. We fry our meat and then take the meat up and then fries the bread in the grease. We have coffey and sugar though I bought my canteen full of syrup. But they are all gone now. You said that you had beans and pie for dinner. I would to God that I could eat with you but you see how it is. Tell all the boys that I am sorry for them. Tell Pole and Sarah to write to me soon and tell them that Dave is in the hospital with the measels. He looks bad. Tell Moten and Ad that I want to read another just such a letter as this was. I can't compose my mind enough to write with much satisfaction but you can guess at what I can't write. I don't know yet what kind of clothes I will need for I don't know when or where we will be moved but if we go up in Va I will need a long frock tailed coat to come to my knees or lower for it is bad to stand out in the rain without good clothes. I stood the other night when it was raining hard. I thought of my old feather bed at home. Tell the folks to quit writing about Liz Carrel being married for we are getting tired of hearing of it. Return my compliments to all that sent them to me and tell the girls that is inquiring about me that I would like to see them very well but I can't for it is Dixie Land I am sustaining and I will live or die on the Frontiers of Dixie. I just saw enough of the Yankeys to know that it is all the remedy to keep it. Tell Lizabeth howda for me. I can't write to all of you individually but I want you all to consider yourselfs included. Ben Gholston is our Captain. We had our election yesterday. Ben Gober was our candidate. Ben got 54 votes and Gober got 18 votes. I wish I could write as good letters as you all can but I am confused so I hardly know what I am writing so you must all put up with this till the next time. Out of so many of you it looks like I could get a letter! Remaining your son and brother truly till Death.

To Susan Landers and Brothers and Sisters

Richmond, Va
Sept the 5th 1861
My dear Mother, Brothers, and Sisters

With pleasure I seat myself this morning to write you a few lines which leaves me tolerable well but only tolerable. Saturday night I was taken with a sick stomach. I was in a terrible condition till Sunday evening but I feel much better today. I think I will be well in a few days. I truly hope when these lines comes to hand they will find everyone of you well. I have nothing new to write only we expect to be called to Manasses Junction in a few days. The Col has sent his horse off to get him shod this morning to be ready though if we are called to go we can't start but about 7 or 8 hundred men of regiment for there is so many of them sick. I feel mighty weak and bad but if they was to start this evening I would go with them. I received your letter the other day and was glad to hear from you but I sent an answer by McKinney. Tell me in your next letter what you done with that old blanket you got from him. We drawed some money this morning. We privates drawed 7 dollars and 70 cents and the officers accordingly. We only drawed from the time we left the mountain till the 1st day of September. We won't draw no more till the first day of December. Then we will draw 33 dollars apiece. I am getting very well satisfied here but yesterday while I was so bad off I did wish I was at home on the bed but I past off the time in my tent the best I could. Silas Cadle of Capt Muthren's company died yesterday with a relapse of the measels. He thought he was about well and worked in the rain and caught cold and died in a few hours. All the boys seems to be anxious to go to the fight. Benjamin Gholston is our captain now. You can just all think what you please about Capt. Richardson and his company that he has forsaken while we think the same. We are looking for our recruits everyday and some brandy and some of our clothes. Mamma don't be grieving about me because we have to leave here. It may be possible that I may go all through and never get a scratch. I want you to try to reconcile yourself to the hand of Providence. I was so glad to hear that the neighbors had not forgotten my absence and to hear that you had friends to assist you in your work. I want you to write as soon as you get this. Probably it may get here before we leave and if it don't it will follow me and write another good long letter like that other one. I was sorry to hear of little Henry getting burnt. I would like to be where I drempt I was last night. I was at home and far from Howell Cobb. I went to see Bill Miner to give my respects to all my friends. Tell them howda for me. I would a liked to bin at old Sweetwater yesterday but I reckon there was not many there, only old mean ladies! Tell the little mule and my filly howdy for me. You wanted me to write what we had to cook in. We have a frying pan and a skillet and a camp kettle. So tell all the settlement boys that I would like to see them shoulder their guns with us. We will draw our guns tomorrow but there is many of this regiment that wont be able to use them. But I hope I will be there. There has been about 15 or 20 died in the course of a week. There was 6 died in one day. Dave Cruse has got well. Arch and Lige is well. Jo Waldrop is getting better. He will start home when he gets able to travel. Tell Pole I couldn't keep from laughing but I was sorry too when I heard of our bottom five being washed away. I just know how he cussed Garner's sawmill. I wish I could a bin there to help put it up. Elbert says he wished me and him and Pole was at the Berth Spring setting in the shade but he can't get his wish. It is mixed uncertainty whether we ever will see that old spring or not. Tell N.B. and Moten to write and not to wait for me to for I have a bad chance. Mamma I want you to try to sell that mule and try to keep my filly and don't let her go to nothing for I may need her some day. I think I can see the Big Officers a fixing to leave here but they would not tell us to save our lives. W.T. Smith is nearly well. He sends his best respects to you all. I have met up with a heap of my acquaintances and some of my connections here. I saw some boys out of the settlement of Uncle Thom Doster. He and family is well. There is one of Uncle John Landers grandsons in this regiment. He said they are all doing tolerable well. Uncle John has got the fever but not dangerously bad. Mamma I would like to take one good talk with you, I never did want to talk with anybody as bad in my life. But if I don't get to see you in a long time I will have the more to talk about then. Mr. and Mrs. Shamblee I thank them for their cheering words. Return the same for me. The people of Richmond is very kind to us. There is some ladies now in our camp with some nourishment for the sick. They depend on the Georgia boys. Them ladies that you were inquiring about and wanted to know their names. Well their names is Sarah and Katy Hix. They send their respects to you all. They say they now have got a smart sister. I make out like I think there is nobody like them and they think a heap of me! I can hear of them talking about me. Tell all the Gwinnett girls howda for me. I would like to see them. Tell them I am in fine spirits but I don't want all of them to marry while I am gone for I must have a Gwinnett girl yet. Tell Harriet that I will try to do what she said for me to do but Jeff Davis is a fine man. Tell the children and Dan that I have not forgot them. Car conduct yourself well though I know you will but there is disgustful people here. Tell Lizabeth and the children howda for me. Pink is well. You wanted to know who was in my mess. Arch, Lige, Bob, Thom Matthews, Jim and Ben Traynham, John Walas, and Dave Cruse. Dave McGinnis has got the measels but is nearly well again. Tell Paulina I would like to hear from her. Ad I want you and Moten to move to the old house before the dead of winter and get shed of old Bill. Sell or swop him for a cow or wagon or something else. Tell Eli Matthews I received his letter and was glad to hear from him but his reports is not true for I went and asked Julius Boen if he was dead and he said not nor old Scott aint dead neither. Old Linkon is not took a prisoner so that report was not true. Tell Eli I will write if I have the chance but if I don't for him to take this for an answer. Tell him I could tell him a heap if I could see him. Tell Bill Matthews to write Bill Carel. Mamma I have always done all I could for you and would yet if I had the chance so I have got more money than I need at this time and for fear I will get it stold or get killed and the Yankeys got it, I will send you a little. Maybe it will do you some good. I'll send it to let you know that out of what I've got you are welcome to some of it. I had rather you would have it than the Yankeys or the rogues. I will send you two dollrs which leaves me with 15 dollars and 50 cents and some in the treasury yet which I think I can make out. It is with pleasure that I do this but I owe you more for your kindness to me than I'll ever be able to pay till the day of death. So I must close my letter hoping that it wont be the last one. I want to hear from you. Write how the Bottom land looks and how that little young peel of corn looks and if you have had any potatoes to eat or not and if the new ground has come out. So no more only tell Sarah and little Pole howda for me. I am a solger for the War. If we had followed our Captain we woulda been in Gwinnett but he was a solger for money. So farewell Dear Mother, Brothers, and Sisters.

E.P.Landers to Susan Landers

Richmond, Va
Sept 11 1861
Dear Mother,

The recruits landed here this morning. We was all glad to see them but was much gladder to receive our things and that old brandy that was sent. You never saw boys as glad in your life as we was. It found us that was sent to all well but it made me think of old Gwinnett mighty strong. We have nothing new since yesterday when I wrote that other letter. We are all as lively as you please. The recruits looks like they was scared. They are not used to our fare. We are getting used to it now. My Respected Mother I went up in town today and got my ambertype taken which I will send to you and I want you to keep this one and give that one you have got to Pole and N.B. but I want you to keep this one for me and believe it to be the same boy that left you. This one cost 3 dollars but I have got about fifteen dollars yet which I think will do me. Today if I ever did feel good it is now but I would liked to aheard from you in a letter. I have not had time to try my drawers on yet but I will save them till cold weather. Mamma I want you to keep my picture as long as you live and show it to all the girls. Tell them that it is a Va Ranger. I give three dollars for it but you won't take 100 dollars for it when you get it! It is just like me now so you can guess how I look. It tells the girls and you all howda for me. It can't talk with you but if I was there I could. Tell Pole to take that old one and keep it till I come home to look at it. Write what you think of it. Look on the cartridge box and you will find my name which was put there with a lead pencil. Arch and Lige has got theres taken too. Both are in one case which cost 4 dollars. I would send you all something if I could for these great presents which you sent but I can't. I will send this by a man going from here this evening to his Lawrenceville home. I must fix it up in such a hurry that I don't expect you can read it. So keep this picture My Dear Mother for it is just like I am now. I would like to have yours but I can't get it. I couldn't take care of it if I had it. I want to know who made my cap. All the others wants it. I would not take a dollar for it. So give my love to all of the

Gwinnett friends. I want to hear of you smiling when you get this. Remember that it is a son of yours who is in the noble cause of his country who will willingly stay with it till death if needed. So let the Sweetwater girls see it. Tell Henry that it is Eel. So farewell dear friends. I know you are my friends. I return my sincere thanks too for the presents. Farewell dear Mother.

Susan Landers from E.P. Landers.

Richmond, Va
Sept 15th 1861
My Dear Mother,

This Sabbath morning I feel like if I can't be with you I will speak to you in the way of lines. These lines leaves me well and truly hoping that they may find you all well too. Mother I have not much to write only I will have to leave this place next week. We will go to Yorktown about 75 miles from this place. We expect to have to take Fortress Monroe. They say that there are forty thousand Yankeys there. The companies that has got guns is ordered to march right away but our company has not drawed no guns yet. We will draw them this week. We draw the old fashioned musket. Mamma I received them things that you sent to me and was proud of my cap. I have got more clothes than I can tote if we have to march by land but we will go on the steamboat to Yorktown. It is on the seaside. We will get to see the Big Body of water. You stated that you had a good crop of potatoes. I was glad to hear of it. Yesterday I was sick and did not feel like eating what we had to eat and I slipped out and found an old Negro with some good baked potatoes and I give him 5 cts for one of them and it was so good. It made me think of our patch. I want you to write whether you got that ambrotype I sent you or not. Tell Pole to keep that old one. Mamma I want you to take special care of it till I come home. Let that be long or short. I would be there today to spend the day with you all but I am here in the hot sun in my tent and the rest of the boys is sweeping the yard. We are badly crowded of a night. There is six to a tent. We are so badly scroughed that we have to get up and go out of doors to turn over but we do the best we can. Tell Moten that I received his brandy with pleasure. Return my thanks for me. I wish you had your bottle again. I was glad to see the old bottle as well as the brandy. Mamma I want you to write how you saved your fodder and how much you have saved. I want you to take care of yourself for I am out of your reach. There has two of the Lawrenceville Co died since we come here. Their names was Cadell and Underwood. Underwood died yesterday with the measels. I have not bin sick only with the diarrhea but I am looking every day when I will be. Nicholas

Shamblee is now in Richmond sick. He is at a hotel. I have not got the chance to go to see him yet. Asa Wright saw him. Bob is going to see him today. Mamma if I go down to Yorktown I will be where there's thousands of Yankeys and if I get into a row with them and they kill me, let it rest on your mind with honor to think that your youngest son died in defense of his country that we might still be a free people. There is many difficulties and trials to undergo here but I prefer it before subjugation. All the boys is getting better in our Co but Lt. Gober and he is very bad off. W.T. Smith looks like a skeleton though he is getting well. Dave Cruse is well. Dave McGinnis is getting well of his ear. Car I have not got time nor room to say nothing to you only be a good girl. Tell all my brothers and sisters and little nieces howda for me and my Connections and friends in general. I receive a letter from old Gwinnett very often but I hear nothing new. I received 3 letters when the recruits came. Arch and Lige and Dave sends their love to you all. Write how all the girls looks and if they have many beaus now. Tell them to wait for us solgers for the Virginia girls don't suit us. So I must close for Pink wants to fill the other side. Mamma I shall never forget the last time I saw you and all the rest of my people. Thom Cobb's Legion has just now past going to Yorktown. Dan Plaster and Jim Brockman is in it so I will close. Farewell to you all. So no more, only remains your son as ever

E.P.Landers to Susan Landers at home

Richmond, Va
Sept 21st 1861
My dear Sister Caroline,

I will write you a few lines with much gratification from your short words to me. These lines leaves me well and hearty and trusting that they may find you well. I am in a poor condition for writing this evening but I will write some. I would like to see you the best in the world. I just want to tell you all about the fun. Car I want you to write to me and write about everybody and everything for I love to read your letters. Car if I never see you again let wisdom be your guide and recollect that I am your friend and well wisher. Remember that you had a brother that laid down his life for your honorable rights so let Patriotism encourage your feelings. Live a prudent and moral life for if we go down to Yorktown and get into a difficulty with the Yankeys they may tug me. Car he is just got well of the measels and Bill Dyer says for you to keep his fiddle till he comes home. Car tell Miss Jane that I love her yet. Give my best respects to all the girls and tell them that I have not forgot none of them. Tell Paulina that I look at the left side of my coat and think of her. The sewing has not ripped yet.

Give my respects to the Poles and Sarah. Tell Sarah that Dave has been sick nearly ever since he has been here with his head but he is getting well. Give my entire respects to Elizabeth and Harriet and their family. Give my best love to all Uncle Eli and family and to James Garner and tell him that I wish that I could be there to hope him to dam up his dam again but he will have to get it done without me. So I must close for the want of time. Round is the ring that has no end. I send my love to you my friend.

E.P.Landers to his sister H.C.Landers

Note: The sewing on Eli's coat as mentioned in the letter was probably referring to some kind of "name tag" that was sewn on a soldier's coat in the event of his being killed on the battlefield and there being no one there to identify the body.

Richmond, Va
Sept 21st 1861
To Moten and Ad and Henry,

      My dear friends I will send a word to you. Ad you don't know my feelings towards you all. We will leave this place in a few days but I don't much care for I am bedeviled nearly to death so that I don't care how soon we fight it out. Moten I can only say howda to you. That is with as gooder feeling towards you as if I had written a whole column. But the drum is beating for drill and everybody has to steer. Moten I would like to see you very well. Say howda to little William Henry. I want to see you so bad that I don't know what to do. I want you to write soon as you get this for I want to hear from you all before I leave this place for I may not hear from you and more for the Yankeys is as thick as hops down about where we are going. I will send this letter by Mr. Hutchins to Yellow River. I am in such a hurry that you must excuse my bad writing. Tell John W.,Shamblee that I saw Nick the other day. He is getting well. He talks like getting a furlough to come home on when he gets able to travel. So I must close for this time. Write soon. I'd like to see William Henry walking. Tell him to not stump his toes. So no more only remaining your brother as ever.

E.P.Landers for the War. Goodby

Richmond, Va
Sept 21st 1861
My Honored Mother,

    With pleasure I resume my seat to write you a few lines to let you know that I am well at this time truly hoping that these few lines may find you all well. W.P.Mason received a letter from Liz this morning. We was glad to hear from you. I have nothing new to write. Times is very good here with plenty to eat and nothing to do but we are looking everyday when we will get the job. We are still at Richmond but we are looking everyday when we will start to Yorktown. The Vice President made us a speach the other evening. He said that he would insure us to be well armed in the course of the next week. Then we will march immediately and I feel willing to go. I have just laid around here like Brutus till I don't care for little things. Mamma it has been some time since I received a word of consolation from you only them few words which Car sent in Pinks letter. It made me think a heap of her. I want you when one of you writes for all of you to put in a word. I want you to write as soon as you get this. Don't wait. Write if you ever got that ambertype I sent by Mr. John Mills and write if you think it favors me or not and if N.B. has got my old one or not and tell him that he owes me a letter for it and I shall look for it to come. I want you to write if you got them two dollars that I sent or not and write everything that you know. Write a long satisfactory letter and if you can't sent it in one letter send it in two. Tell all to write. I dream about you all nearly every night. I drempt Mamma had come to see me and I was going about over Richmond with you but I hope that the day will come when it will not be in dreams that I will be with you when we will set down round your table to eat in independent peace for that is the only way that I ever expect to eat with you again. My dear Mother this is a dreadful life but I feel reconciled to it for I believe that we are on the right side of the question. They brought in 2000 more Yankeys the other day but that is nothing for there is more prisoners in Richmond now than they know what to do with. Mamma save all the fodder and hay that you can for I want you to keep my filly if you can possibly do it for if we whip the devils and I get back home I will need her. Jo Waldrop has gone home. He started this morning. He got a discharge. W.T. Smith is most well. One of the Lawrenceville boys died this morning. His name was Kemp. There has four died out of our company.

    Mamma I think about you every hour in the day. I just think about you working so hard without me till I hardly can stand it. It was hard enough when I was there to help you but you must do the best you can. It is hard for you to do without me and for me to lie on my blanket but I freely do it for our freedom. Tell all my connections howda for me and all the girls. Tell Miss Juley and Miss Margret Hopkins howda for me and tell them I thank them for their compliments to me so Mamma well wishes to you. I must close. Farewell my dearest friend. So no more only remaining yours truly.

E.P.Landers to Susan Landers at home

Richmond, Va
Sept 24th 1861
My Dear Mother, Brothers, and Sisters and all,

I take pleasure in answering your kind letter which came to hand yesterday and found me well but I am not well today. I was taken last night with a throwing up. I was very bad off through the night but I feel much better this morning. I think I will get well in a few days. I hope this letter will find you all well. I have nothing new to write but I will write every time you do. We are here yet and there is not as much talk about leaving now as there was when I wrote my last letter. We did have orders to leave rite away but that was counter-manded. I think that they will start us before long though we may not leave in a good while for the Yankeys is watching this place like a hawk does a chicken. They think if they could just get this place they would have the Confederacy whipped but I don't think that they will ever get it for there is about 20,000 solgers round in this vicinity which can be at their post in a few hours. But there is not near as many here now as was when we first come here. Cobbs Legion is gone to Yorktown. There was several in it that I was acquainted with. Dan Plaster and Jim Brockman is in it. Your letter give me great satisfaction. I was glad to hear of you getting your fodder pulled but was sorry to hear of the corn being so sorry. But maybe if you will save of it you can make out on it. Tell Eli that I will remember him for his kindness to you and James Garner too for it is the best news that I have had yet. You said for me to take good care of number one but I will tell you that is all the way I will try to do for its every man for himself here. You said that everytime you lay down you thought how I was lieing but don't you trouble yourself about that. But I will tell you how it is. We got some pieces of plank and put a floor in our tent but we've not got but 4 blankets in our tent. We spread down one of them and cover with the others. It is a hard bed but we do very well and as for what we have for breakfast we have bread and meat and coffey that is good enough sometimes. I buy some little nourishment. I have bought some milk a time or two but it is not good like it is at home. You can get it for 5 cts a pint. We cant buy a pound of butter for less than 80 cts. We have bought one pound in our mess. Your letter said that Pole and Moten wanted to come so bad. If they will take my advice they will not come till they are needed worse than they are now. They keep bringing in the Yankeys ever once in a while. We have got more of them now than we no what

34

to do with. I think that a good many of them is glad to be took. You wanted to know if I got that brandy and things. I got all of them and liked them mighty well. You said that I write such good letters but I don't think that I ever read a better letter than yours was. It is more satisfaction to me to read one of your letters than anything comes before. I can just think who wrote it and where it come from but I hope the day will come when our conversation will not be kept up by mail but with our tongues. But we are in for the War and there is no prospect for peace as I can see but we don't know no more about it than you do. You may think because I am in Va that I know all about the war but I tell you I don't for we don't get the chance to run about. We just have to stay rite round the camp. You bragged on my picture till I begin to think I do look well. Tell Pole that I will still look for that letter. Tell Ad that she surely don't want to see me any worse than I do her. I would like to take some long civil talks with you all for there is no civility in camps. They are always hollowing or playing the fiddle and all such foolishness tell it has wore me out of patience. Give my best love and respects to Dan and Harriet and all the family. Tell them I want to see them so bad. Give my love to Pole and Sarah. I was glad to see them few lines that Pole wrote. Tell Liz howda and Charles and Maryann too. Car I never will forget you. I want you to write to me when you can and write all the news. Tell Miss Paulina that I thank her for her well wishes towards me but tell her that there is not much comfort in a camp life. Tell her to be sure and make that dress and then write to me. Give my respects to George Shamblee and family and tell him to write to me. Tell Rachel Shamblee that I saw Nicholas the other day. He is getting well. W.T. Smith is most well. He will come back to the camp in the morning. Lt. Gober is very weak and feeble. He has been very bad off. Mamma let all the girls look at my ambertype. Tell them to not forget the substance of it for I cannot never forget them. Tell Sarah that if we can me and Dave will go to town this evening and Dave will get his picture and send it home. Mamma you said if I wanted a blanket you would send it to me but I will not send for it till cold weather, till we see what old Cobb will do for us. I would like to sleep a night or two on my bed in the upper house but I don't believe I will do it . I said I had nothing to write and so I hant writ much but I must close. Mamma don't be uneasy about me being sick for I feel a heap better. I reckon it was just a little sick brash. I close with the best of wishes to you if on earth we meet no more oh may we meet in a better country and I hope I will be remembered and not forgotten. Arch and Lige and Dave Cruse is well so nothing more. Only I remains your son as ever and will till death. May God Bless us all. So farewell. Write soon.

E.P. Landers to Susan Landers at home

Richmond, Va
October 6th 1861
My Dear Mother and Sister,

    This being Sunday morning as nothing else to do, I will write you a few lines to let you no that I am well and trusting that this may find you all well. I have nothing new to write. I am as hearty as I ever was in my life and am well satisfied as any of the rest of the boys. We have had a very serious time since this time yesterday morning for we have witnessed the death of one of our fellow solgers to wit Thomas Sanders. He died with a relapse of the measels. He got most well of them and exposed hisself in the rain. His relapse was very hasty to death. He only lasted 5 days the last round. He died last night about 1 o'clock. It was a very solemn occasion. He was out of his senses all the time. I was detailed to wait on him 24 hours. It almost wearied me down for he was trying to skip off all the time. He said he was going home but the poor fellow will return home with his eyes closed. Asa Wright will come home with him. The Co all seemed to throw in their little mite to send him home with all pleasure and I for one did. I put in 75cts. It was heart rending to hear the bitter cries of him. The poor fellow called his Mother often. He died very hard indeed. There is no hopes of his Eternal rest for he swore till the last but Eternal woe must shorely be his portion but it is not for us to know for the one who made him is able to save him. John Sanders is down with the measels now and it is doubted wheather he ever will get well or not. The sick sees hard times for they are lying in the hospital tents on some straw. God forbid that I shall ever spend my last days in such a place for it is awful to see the sick groaning on any such place. Enough of that.

    I am looking for a letter from some of you and I would be glad to see it come for it has been some time since I have heard from you. As long as I can get letters from you or any of my friends I can do very well but when I can't hear from you all I begin to feel a long ways from home and that you all have forgotten me though I no that you never will forget me. I want you and Car to write when you can for I read your letters with great pleasure. I don't no whether you like to read my letters as good as I do yours or not. If I knew that you did I would write oftener than I do. I would like to see you all but I don't no whether I ever will see you or not. But I never expect to see you till I can land home in honor for that is the only way that I ever expect to see old Gwinnett. I expect to stand my hand in the Cause as long as I can for I am now sold to Jeff

Davis and I expect to serve him till he discharges me in honor or until I die. I saw him yesterday evening. He was on the finest horse you ever saw. His head is as white as cotton. We all fair tolerable well here. We get plenty of bread and beef to eat and some old red coffey and sugar and we buy some potatoes and molasses. My mess all throwed in and bought 1 gallon of molasses yesterday. We had good cake and coffey and old red molasses and fried taters for breakfast. But we don't have a clean tablecloth to put on of a Sunday morning! It is every man git his handfull and stand round and eat it and if a fellow stands back he gets none. We are yet at old Richmond and it is very uncertain when we will leave. Us privates can tell you nothing about that for we don't no.

Mamma it has not bin quite two months since I saw you and Car but it looks like it has been twelve. But I come home of a night occasionally but you no that you can make nothing of a dream, only a dream. But it does me some good to dream of seeing you Mamma. I want you to send me a good blanket or a coverlid for the nights is getting cold and we have not got enough of bedclothes. Arch will send for one. Send them by Asa Wright when he comes back and if you can get them ready. I want you to send me another flannel shirt and drawers. Tell Tob or Moten one to send me a good pair of buckskin gloves for I will need them and they cost a dollar and fifty cents here. My shoes lasted finely. They are as good as ever only they need half soling. It will cost me a dollar and twenty five cents to get them halfsoled or four dollars for a new pair. All this is the truth. Mamma I want you to write all the news about the crop and stock and the neighbors. Tell all my friends to write to me. The question of Peace is talked of here but I don't no when that thing will occur, but not soon I do not think. They have little rounds ever once in a while up in northwestern Virginia. I think that we will be with them before long to take a part with them and I don't much care when we start for I have just got the "don't cares" the worst kind and all the boys seems to be in the same fix. Arch and Lige and Dave and Pink and Bob is all well. Tell W.R.Miner to come over and stay till bedtime with me and tell me all about the girls. Tell him to write. Give my love and compliments to Mis Mary Smith and to all the girls. Tell them to look at my Ambrotype and think of the original. Tell them that it is a Confederate Solger. Show it to Miss Margret and Subey Hopkins and to Miss Emily R. Tell them to kiss it and then tell me of it. Enough of that. Mamma write if you think you will make enough corn to do you or not and how big is the biggest potatoes that you have got. Give my best respects and love to Dan and Harriet and all the children. I want to see them so bad. Tell Eliza and the children howda for me. I can't write to you all. One letter includes all so I must close for I want to write to Ad and Moten. Mamma take care of my mare. So nothing more for this time. Excuse this letter and I will do better next time. I remains yours very truly as ever.

E.P.Landers Your Son to Susan Landers

Richmond,VA
Oct 9th,1861
My dear old Mother

This day I take great pleasure in answering your letter that I read this morning and also happy to receive your affectionate features [Photograph]. I read your letter with the greatest pleasure though it did not come to hand as you desired it to for I was not well, though not very bad off. I reckon it is the cold. I can't hardly write for my hand is So numb though I think in a few days I will be ready for service but if I dont I intend to go out to a private house for I dont think that the hospital tent ~is fit for me to stay in as long as I can do better. I havent got much to write and I am feeling so bad you need not expect to much of a letter but I will do the best I can manage. It made me feel awful bad when I received your ambertype. It looked so natural and just to think who it was and where the original of it was, money couldnt get it. W.T. Smith put it in his trunk. He says he will take care of it till the Yankeys take it from him. I was not looking for it Mamma.

I reckon you have heard of Tom Sanders being dead. Now his brother John Sanders is dead. He died yesterday morning. He is up in town in a vault. They have sent his father word to come after him if he wants to. Both of them went just alike. They were out of their head all the time. John only lasted 2 days after his relapse. He was getting well and he went out and got drunk and then drunk as much cold water as he wanted. The next morning he could not walk nor never did again. He died in the same tent that Thom did. We can have no hopes for their eternal welfare for they both swore till the last but that is with them and their Maker. It is not for us to say. Enough of that for it is bad enough. We are very doubtful of Alfred Jim a living for he is very low.

Mamma I was glad to hear that you have saved so much fodder. I think that you have got enough to do. You give my best respects to all that hope you and tell them that I will not forget them though I cannot do anything for them now. I am glad to hear from my filly. You must write some about her everytime. Mamma I would like to see you but I dont know how long it will be till I do for the infernal Yankeys intends to wipe us out as they first said but I dont think that they ever will do it for I think the Lord is with us and if he be for us who need to be agin us. As the Bible says the wicked fleeth when no man pursueth. It proved so in the cowardly rout at Manassas.

The weather is very indifferent now. It is cold and cloudy and has been for several days. Night before last there was the hardest rain fell that I ever heard fall. All the boys was put to it badly but us in our tent did very well for we are better fixed than any of them. We have got pieces of plank and put a floor in it and me and Arch went out in the country and got some straw. The water just ran through their tents and wet them and their blankets. Some of the tents blew down and of all the times they had with it but I kept nearly dry. We are crowded badly of a night. You wanted to know if I needed any shoes. I don't need them now but I soon will and they cost six or seven dollars here. If you can I want you to send me a pair of homemade ones. I feel so bad I will quit till morning.

[Eli is not able to finish his letter but wants it sent and I will close it by signing his name.]

E.P.Landers by E.M.McDaniel signer

Richmond,Va
October 1861
My Respected Sister
     I am very tired a writing but I will write you a few lines. You said that you had never received but one letter from me yet but every letter I send home it is to you all. You was telling me of the fun you and Add had. I dont think it was much fun. You had better be careful she will hurt some of you. I dont think my little Jane is very dangerous that one at home and I am not much afraid of my other little Jane. Give her my best respects and compliments. H.C. I was with you this morning about daylight but the Legion drum beat waked me up. I just had got home but the sound of the drum brought me back to Camp again but I hope the day will soon come when I will be at home so the drums cant bring me back. Excuse this sorry letter for I never was as tired a writing. You must do the best you can this summer and don't work too hard. I will close for this time. I want you to write when you can.

E.P.Landers to H.C.Landers

Mrs. R.A. Hutchins
Dear Sister,

I will write you a few lines to let you know that I have respects for you. I read your letter with great pleasure but I have nothing now to return in reply. I was very sorry to hear of your bad luck losing your milk cow. It looks like your lot is hard. I dont know what you will do now. There is no chance to buy one at the present prices but as you say, it is best to hold a high head and a stiff neck for it will do no good to take things to heart too much. I was just thinking the other day about Sweetwater graveyards. I know it would make me feel bad to go over it and see the silent tombs of so many of my friends whom I have been with so often. How thankful I aught to be that I have not been numbered with them yet. Add you must do the best you can for yourself. I wish I had something to write. I have been writing nearly all day. I am in a cramp sitting so long. Give my love to all the connections and friends. So I must close and cook some of my ham for dinner.

E.P.Landers to R.A.Hutchins

Gwinnett County, Ga
October 1861
Dear Son,

I take pleasure in writing to you this evening. This leaves all well but me and I got my arm broke. I went up to Bird Martins the day before he was to start to take the letter for him to take and he was gone to Miss Fords to take a start and I was hurrying back to send them to him and up there on the red hill between her and Lill Miners I slipped down and cotch bac~ on my arm and broke it but I think one bone is broke and the other cracked but dont you grieve about that for my friends will gather my corn. I would not a went to McCartys to get my picture taken. I was a going to Atlanta to get it taken but I was afraid you would get killed and never get to see me and if it fades out let me know it and I send you anotther if you want it and can take care of it though I cant shortly for my present tax is 4 dollars besides the war tax. It will be some 8 or 10 dollars. We are trying to sell the mule. Yancey Cruse.says he thinks we can get 50 dollars for it. He is to speak to Cruse about it though money is very hard to come by. We will try to sell it at some price for our corn crop will come off short this year. You wanted to know how large the largest potatoes we got. We have got some as large as your leg but all the rows next to the ditch soured. I do wish you had some of them Bird would not take nothing to eat to you boys. He said he was not allowed to take nothing but clothing. If Asa Wright will take such things we will send you all such things we have got. We will send you some sweetbread and potatoes and a coverlid and three quarts of brandy. We could not get your pants ready and as for flannel there aint none to be had about here. We will send your pants when we do your shoes or boots and I want to know which you had ruther have boots or shoes. Write which soon and I will get Tect to make you some and as for the oilcloth we all don't know what about them yet. If times was not so hard you should have arry thing you wanted. Bacon is 30 cts a pound, molasses 60 cts, paper 50 cts a quire and none hardly at that. Coffee is 2 pounds to the dollar but our country don't make much use of it. Calico is 20 and 25 cts a yard but everybody is wearing cotton dresses. Your sow had 5 nice pigs. Our hogs all looks well. Your mare looks mighty well. She is so petted. Moten has not broke your steers yet but will shortly. Pole and Moten is gathering our corn on the piece next to the Meeting House. It never made quite 4 loads but that is good to what a heap people up land is. Eli you needn't to be uneasy about us for we are surrounded with Christian friends while you are up there with those Yankeys and if we never meet in this world I want us to try to meet in a better one. Ben Gholston says you and Bob Miner is two of the nicest boys in camp and I was glad to hear it. Me and Moten has not made no arrangements about our crop yet but when we do you will know how it made. Eli I do want to see you so bad. I wish my son well. It was heart rendering to hear the bitter crying of Mr. Sanders people at the burying. It made me feel awful. I just thought what if it was you. My arm is mending. It is set so good. "Eel", me and Elizabeth had sweetcakes and large potatoes and butter all ready to send to you and Pink but Wright couldnt take them but we will send them in one or two weeks by express. Goodby, my child.

Susan Landers to E.P.Landers

Portion of letter—Undated

Tell A.W. that our sharp shooters is all fixed up now. Lieut Martin and Simmons is now Captain and Captain Hutchins is Colonel of the battalion and John W.King is Captain of the company from Cobbs Legion. We will have another Lieut to elect I reckon to fill the vacancy of Lieut Martin. The Capt and first Lieut and 4 sergeants from the Hutchins Guards joined the sharp shooters. They will have to elect 2 Lieutenants. Tell A.W. to not think hard of me for not writing him a letter for we are looking to have to march all the time. We keep our things ready. Tell him that Capt. A.B. got his certificate. It is all right. Tell Aunt Siby that me and E.M. could take in her churn of milk and butter and not think hard of it!lTell her I am much obliged for her sympathy though it done us no good for we did not get the milk nor eggs. I will close for I think from the movements of everything we will leave directly. Remember if I march further from home my love and thoughts is left behind with you so nothing more. Write soon.

E.P.Landers to Susan Landers

Gwinnett County, Ga
October 1861
My Dear Brother,

I take great pleasure in writing to you. This leaves me well and I look as well and better than I ever did in my life. I do hope this may find you well and the the Flint Hill Greys as well. "Eel" if you knowed how bad I wanted to see you you would run away and come home. "Eel" I will tell you about the mule. It come in the house today. It is the tamest thing you ever saw. We got your letter you sent by Asa Wright. We read it with great pleasure but was sorry to hear of you losing one of your fellow soldiers. We all went to his burying. I tell you it was solemn times with us all. There was a large congregation there but they did not open the coffin let us see him. He was buried at Sweetwater. I intend to keep his grave nice. I want to know if you want to be brought home if you die. I want you to. I don't care what it costs. Eel I want to know whether you got them apples I sent to you or not. I sent them in your coat pocket because there was 8 of them. You said you didn't know whether we liked to read your letters as good as you do ours. We like to read them letters. I expect Eel the girls all looked at your picture. They all thought it was so pretty. Mat Mc kissed it and so did Elly Nash and Paulina says it is just like you. There was good many at Meeting but the young men was so guilty they stayed outdoors. All the girls had on cotton dresses. Ad says when she gets paper she will write you a long letter. Harriet sent you this coverlid. She says she had rather you had it than to keep it. She says she wants to see you so bad. She says if you feel any change in life she wants you to let us know it. She says she is in hopes you do. Dan said if he had paper he would a wrote you a letter. He sends his respects to you. He says he recons Asa Wright will tell you what he is doing. All the connections and friends sends their respects to you. Extend our respects to Mr. Hix's family. Also tell the girls I will look for a letter from them. Tell them I want to know how they like the Ga boys. I never can forget them. Tell them I would like to see them. Their names is highly esteemed in this settlement. Eel write a piece to Mary Smith and put it in our letter. You and Lige is the ones she wants to hear from. It is almost night. I must hurry if I could write as good letters as you I wouldn't

42

mind writing. Tell all your mess howdy for me. Eel you don't know what a tender feeling I have for you. I want you to serve the Lord as well as Jeff Davis for I hope when you return you will be a Christian soldier. Tell Lige howdy for me and Arch and Dan Davis. Tell Dave I want him to write me a letter also Ben and Jim Mathews. It is so dark I cant see how to write anymore but maybe you can read it. Tell Bob Miner to write and all the rest. Liz says tell you howdy. Tell Pink I would like to see him. Eel you are the bravest Landers of all and I respect you for it! We will send you a pillow I reckon.

Caroline Landers to E.P.Landers

Eel I want to see you very bad but I hope that peace will be made and you will get home again. There would be great joy. We are well and hope this may find you well and all of the Flint Hill Grays. Eel, Henry was mighty proud of his money. I kiss him for you but I rather it woulda been you. Moten says tell you howda. Eel there was a heap of the girls come from the meeting house and saw your likeness. They say it was pretty and says they never will forget you. Adaline Hutchins to E.P.Landers

Richmond, V.
October 13th, 1861
My Dear Mother,

I take this opportunity to write you a few lines to let you know that I am not well at this time, but hope this may find you in better health than it leaves me in. I am sick at this time. I am out in a private house. I dont know what my spell will terminate into but I hope nothing very serious. I am treated as well here as if I was at home and had my mother to wait on me. Its much better than being in camp in them old tents on the ground like many of my fellow soldiers is. Here I have a good feather bed to lie on and much better attention than if I had of stayed in camp. My Captain is very kind to me. He lets Arch of Lige or Pink come and he come to see me himself too. I just stayed in camp till I found out I was going to be sick and I got Lige and Sam Dyer to get me a place and I got a pass to go out and return in two hours and I pitched my place and aint gone back yet but I hope it wont be long till I can be with the rest of the boys. My captain knowed I was not a coming back but he was darent to give me permission to go out to stay. The colonel wont let his men out when they are sick. He says the hospital tents is good enough but I didnt think so. We have lost three men out of our company and I dont believe they would of died if they had of had a feather bed and a good house to lay in and good attention. I am staying at Mr. Pembertons. They are very kind to me. The reason I didnt stay at Mr. Hines is that one of his daughters is sick with the fever and I didnt think I could get very good care there so I must claose. Write soon.

E.M. McDaniel writing for E.P. Landers

Aunt Susan, you neednt to be uneasy about Eli for I think he gets good attention where he is.

Richmond, Va
Oct the 14th 1861
Dear Brother,

I received your letter last night and was proud to hear from you all and to hear that all was well but Mamma. I was very sorry to hear that Mamma had got her arm broken. It is a pity but I hope that the neighbors will attend to her farm till she can use her arm again. Pole, this letter leaves me a little better than I was yesterday though I did not rest as good last night as I did the night before. I sent for the doctor last night but he did not come. He will be here this morning for sure. I hope that I will not have a spell of the fever if I can get the doctor here in time to break it up before it goes too far. Pole, I am at a private house and the people is as clever to me as if I was a kin to them. I am on a feather bed and as many pillows as I want. Arch stayed with me last night. He waited on me like I was his brother but that still aint like it was Mamma but I am well satisfied considering everything.

The report is that we will get our guns today and leave here Wednesday for Yorktown but I don't know whether it is so or not for there is many reports in camp that I don't know when to believe anything. If the Regiment leaves this week I will not be able to go with the boys. I will keep Arch to wait on me if I can for I rather him or Lige would wait on me as anybody else. The Captain will detail him to stay with me if it is in his power to do so. Tell Mamma to not be uneasy about me for I get the best kind of attention from the people that I am staying with and the Capt does all he can for me by sending the boys out to wait on me. The lady of the house put a mustard plaster on my back. I let it stay till it burnt it well and it hope me. Tell Mamma to take good care of her arm and let it get well as soon as possible for she is the dependance and not study about me. Pole I want to see you mity bad but Pole I advise you as a brother to stay at home and take care of your money for I know that money is hard to get in Gwinnett. It will cost you not less than forty five dollars to come and go and that is a heap of money for you to dig out of the ground. Pole keep your money for the use of your family and for Mamma for I know that she is needy. I want you to write to me often. Pink is well. He nearly cried when I read about little Charles. I must close hoping this will find you all well and will write to me soon.

E.P.Landers to Brother Napoleon

Richmond, Va
October 25th 1861
My Dear Mother,

Today I am going to try to write you a letter to let you know how I am. I am getting better. I can walk about in the house now. I have been sick nearly 3 weeks. I was taken with the intermittent fever and I was just getting well of that when I was taken with the measels but they did not hurt me much. My Regiment has left me and gone to Yorktown. They left last Saturday morning about day. The doctors would not let nobody stay with me but I have done very well without them. I reckon that I will go to camp in 3 or 4 weeks if I don't get no backset for I want to be sound when I try it again for I will tell you the camp is a rough place. I would like to see some of you but I reckon there is no chance for money is so scarce. I would get a furlough and come home but there can be no furlough got now. I want you to write as soon as you get this letter and and tell me just what you sent by R.B. Martin for I have never got nothing yet. Asa Wright said that there was a box of things that Mr. Mason brought. He did not know wheather there was anything in it for me or not but he said that there was a coverlid on the top of it. I allowed it was for me. Tell Pole I want to see him mighty bad. Give my love to all for I can't separate them. I am staying with Mr. Pemberton. They treat me as well as they can and they tend to me like I was a child though I have to pay my way and I have not got the money to pay them now but they say to not mind that for if I didn't have a cent they would treat me as well as if I had 1000 dollars! They have took in about 70 solgers since the war began. Mamma don't be uneasy about me for I will do the best I can for myself. Direct your letters to me. Dont have it in care of the Captain. If you do it will go right on to the company before I get it. Dave Haney is at the St.Charles Hospital. Us two is all that was left. N. Shamblee is at the same place yet. I am now sitting and I have sot longer this time than I ever have before. I think all I need now is to take good care of myself and have something to eat which I get plenty of and that is good. W.D. Cruse went off with mumps or he was not well of them. There is 6 Negroes here that wait on me well. No white folks only the old man and woman. I was sorry to hear of you getting your arm broke but I hope it will do well so I must close for I feel so tired. Write just as soon as you get this for I want to hear from you. I have thought of you often since I have been sick but thoughts was all. Tell Car howda so no more at present only I remains your son as ever. So goodby for this time.

E.P.Landers to Susan Landers

Gwinnett County, Ga
Oct the 28th 186Dear Son,

     With much pleasure I seat myself to write you a few lines to inform you that we are all well. My arm is mending. I do hope this may find you in better health than you was when you sent that letter by Bill Cothren. I was so sorry to hear of you being sick. It almost broke my heart. We never received your letter you sent by Bill Cothren till the 23rd of October. Eli I feel so bad about you being sick that I cant hardly write you. My best love and thanks to the people that you stay with. As to the one that stayed with you I am mighty uneasy about you because I can't hear from you. Paiden lost Uncle Ely's letter Arch sent. If you have not written I want you to write as soon as you get this and write how you are and how you have been and all about it. Eli you be sure and don't go to camp too soon and don't drink too much cold water or else you might be brought home like Tom Sanders. I do crave to be there to put my hand on your aching head and to wait on you but I hope that good woman will be a Mother to you. Give her my Love and thanks. I hope the Lord will be your physician. Look un:o Him. I hope He will raise you and let you return home and see us all again. You will hear from us shortly. We will write when we send your shoes. We could not send you anything with Wright, only a half gallon of brandy. It was in the jug with Bob Miners in W.T. Smith's box. I woulda sent you an oilcloth but Jim and Uncle Ely went and got theirs before I knew it and they said when you stand guard Arch and Lige would lend you theirs and I was scarce of money and had to pay the cash for your shoes but I don't mind that I got them from Michels. Old Anderson will make them. The connections and neighbors all seems to be very uneasy about you. They all send their respects to you. I do not hardly know what to write until I hear from you. We sent you a letter by Wright. I want to know if they was gone to Yorktown before Wright got back. Jim Cruse got a letter from H.D. Landers. They was all well. They had got a letter from you and Dave. They said Wealthy had sent you and Dave a pair of pants and says we want to know if you got them or not. We are preparing you a jeans pair of pants and vest. We was a going to send them with the shoes as Wealthy has sent you some we don't know whether you need them or not and if you don't write soon. Before Uncle Ely starts, anything you need send for it for if you think we can get it. My respected son, be sure and take good care of yourself until you get perfectly well. Eli if you ever get well and starts to your company be careful for the report is now that when Mattison Michal got well and started to his company he got took prisoner. I suppose Dick Erwin is a going to Washington Monday week. I want you to call on the Lord and if you feel any evidence let me know it. I do wish I was there to do something for you but as it is I can only pray for you and I hope you have a in my prayers. Bird Martin has just got home. We have not saw him but they say he has not got no letter for us. I suppose he didn't call on you as he come through. He said Wily Hopkins had not been seen nor heard from in a month in Manasses nor Richmond. We all think he is dead or took prisoner and I want you to be conscious how you go about or you might be took. If you do go out on picket guard watch out or the Yankeys will get you. Eli be sure and don't go back to camp too soon. That is my request to you so goodby my child.

From H.C.
Eel, me and Pole went to Sam's burying. They preached his funeral. The connections took it very hard. If you want us to send you any paper write soon as it is hi there. Betsy Ann wishes to be remembered. Goodby for this time. Write soon.

H.C.Landers and Susan Landers

Richmond, Va
Nov 1st 1861
Dear Mother,

This morning I take pleasure in writing to you to let you know how I am today. I am improving though I have had a bad time of it. The doctor did not think that I would get over it but I am getting along finely. I received your letter last night. John Peden stayed with me last night. He said that times are very good in old Gwinnett. Mamma you said that Wealthy had sent me and Dave Cruse some clothing. If she has we never have saw nothing of them and I recon you had better send them pants by Uncle Eli for I may need them and send me a pair of socks if you can. Mamma don't be uneasy about me for I am at a good place. I have good old motherly woman, plenty to eat and that what is good. I can walk about up and down the street right smartly. Yesterday I walked about 200 yards. Tell Uncle Eli to call and see me when he comes. He will find me close by the old fair grounds. Tell him to inquire for the old fair grounds and for Mr. Pemberton and he will soon find me.

Mamma it made me feel bad to read your and H.C.'s letter because you wrote me a letter but I have nothing to write back. I wish I had something that would interest you all. I don't reckon I could get a furlough now and if I could I have not got the money to come home on for I would have to pay half price so I reckon I can't come home. Mamma I have to pay my board here and hain't got but about 3 dollars in my pocket. Though if I was at the Regiment today I could draw 2 months wages. Miss Pemberton says that if I did not have a cent she would still do all she could for me. It will take very near all my wages and all the money I've got to pay my doctor bill and my board. They did not leave anybody to wait on me. Arch thought that they was going to let him but the sargent of the regiment wouldn't let him. But I've done very well without him. But I have not gotten that brandy though I recon they will save it for me in Yorktown.

Mamma don't trouble yourself about me for there is as strong a God here as there is in Georgia. I think that I will be able to go back to camp in 2 weeks if I still keep improving. Give my best respects and love to Harriet and Dan and the children. Tell them I want to see them bad. Tell Liz and the two children I want to see them bad. Rassel William Henry for me. I want to see him so bad. Tell Moten and Ad howda for me. Give my best love and respects to all of the Sweetwater Girls and to all inquiring friends and receive a good portion yourself. I will take good care of myself and do the best I can. So I must close my letter. I hope that I will see you all again. I received a letter from Sarah Norman the other day. It said all was well.

E.P.Landers to Susan Landers

> Though far away in distant clime,
> Where Southern deeds nobly shine,
> Battling against northern crimes,
> Still off to thee my heart inclines.

Gwinnett County, Ga
November 4th 1861
My Dear Child,

I feel like if I can't be with you I wish to speak in the way of lines. This leaves all well. My arm is mending fast. I hope this may find you mending too.

We started a letter to you by Ely and he got as far as Atlanta and he give out but he's going again next Monday. And you said for me to write you as soon as I got your letter. I was mighty glad to hear you was getting better. I sent you a little box of things by Paiden and I wish to know if you received them or not. Ely took the box to Atlanta and left them there. We sent you a butter coverlid and a pair of pants, potatoes, sweetbread and a half quire of paper. He will take them Monday. I reckon there weren't anything in W.J. Morgans box for you. That coverlid was Pink's. We would of sent your things by Rito but we heard he was not allowed to take no box. I was very sorry to hear they would not let no person stay with you. But you said you got good attention from the people you stay with. Give Mr. and Mrs. Pemberton my humble thanks. I hope the Lord will reward them for it. You said you was scarce of money and I expect it will take all you draw to pay your way and if you cannot make out when you go back to your company I will send you some if I can sell my mule. But be sure and don't go back to your company too soon, if you remain weakly. Ely says he is going to bring you home. If I had the money I would come there but he expects to stay there 2 or 3 weeks. I would write more but it is Monday morning and I have to send Caroline to the post office and Ely could not get off last Friday with your letter. I do want to see you mighty bad and talk with you but my child take good care of yourself and don't go to camp too soon. I hope the Lord will be your friend for He is all our dependance. Look to Him for help. I want to know if you have thought of those things. I do crave to see your pleasant face again. I will close for now. Good by if I never see you no more. Write soon and often to me. I could read letters from you all day. Moten hasn't moved yet. We will give you more satisfaction the next time.

Susan Landers to E.P.Landers

Richmond, Va
Nov 15th 1861
My Dear Mother,

This morning I will drop you a few lines to let you know how I am. I am not as well as I was when I wrote my last letter. Since that time I have had a disease nearly like the mumps. It got in my secrets and I thought that I would be ruined. I suffered tremendously though I am now getting over that. I have had a hard time of it. I don't no when I will go back to camp. The Capt sent me word by old man Franklin to stay in Richmond till I got perfectly well for he says where they are there is no place for a sick man. They say it is a very cold wet part of the world. I don't believe that I will be able to stand the camps this winter for they are exposed and sent out on picket two or three miles from the camp on the bank of the waters where the wind can come from a long ways off. The picket says that sometimes they can see the Yankey vessels sailing about away off from the shore. They just can discover them that they are throwing up breastworks.

Bill Elis is here now. He is coming home. He is discharged and says it is tuff times. He says that it takes nearly all of the well solgers for duty. Nun hardly to drill. They have some for picket guard and some to guard round the Regiment and some to work at the breastworks. So I don't think that I can stand it for it is so cold and most always rainy bad weather. I have bin here 5 weeks today. I now owe Mr. Pemberton 20 dollars. I will tell you that it is taking a pore man's pocket change tolerable low. I have not got but 5 dollars and 50 cts in my pocket though I recon that I will draw my wages. I am not near as well as I was two weeks ago. I don't no what I will do for I don't want to go to a hospital for I had nearly as well be in camp but I don't think that Mr.Pemberton will be particular about the money for he's a mighty fine old man. I think that they ought to give me a discharge but they say that a man must have some settled disease. But I am not able for service. I have bin looking for Uncle Ely for the last two days. You said he would start out Monday and this is Friday and he has not come yet. Last night I was the worst fooled. In the night I herd somebody come to the outside door and called to unlock the door. The voice was just like Uncle Ely. I jumped up and opened my room door and unlocked the door and was fixing to shake hands with him and when he stepped in it was one of the boarders that had just bin out in town and was just coming in. I was mad.

Mamma don't you be uneasy about me for I have got as much sense as I ever had but that's not much. I will try to take care of myself the best I can and I have a few friends in Virginia yet if I can just get my health and keep it, things will be alright with me. I hate to hear of you and Car being so troubled about me. It is true that I have bin through the rubs but I hope for better times to come. I would like to be at home to stay till I get well but there is no more furloughs to be given tell after the 4th of January. They have very tight laws in the army. Maw try to reconcile yourself about me for you can't mend the matter. Tell Pole I wish I sould see his crop of corn. There is good crops in Va. Corn is from 55 to 60 cts. Tell Pole that down about Bethel close by Yorktown the Yankeys took possession of a settlement of corn and thought they was doing big things and old General Magruder went and run them off and is now a gathering the corn for us. He has gathered 500 wagon loads. I wish that the President would send us to Savannah where the weather would be warmer and we would be closer home. Times is hard in Richmond. Salt is 25 dollars a sack, beef 12 and a half cts per pound, chickens 30 cts. and butter 40cts. I got a letter from Yorktown the time I got yours. Arch and Lige had the mumps and they was in a bad fix. They was in and out of a house and Dave Cruse is waiting on them. It is a good tight house. If I go to camp and get sick I think I will go to that house and not have to pay so much. They can get good fare in there and be comfortable. Elis says that they are most well now. Give my love to all the connections and to all inquiring friends. Tell them to write. Tell them I am a man now. I will weigh fully 100 pounds! Tell Pole that somebody stole my brandy. Spirits is very high at Yorktown. You have to pay 25 cts a drink and one dollar and 25 cts a qt for brandy. That is very hi drinking! If a man had 500 gallons of peach brandy there or up on the Potomac, he could make a fortune of it. Well I will close for now. Write soon and write how full the corn crib is and how you are managing the hogs and if you have got any pigs and if my sow has ever had any pigs. I want to no all about what is going on so goodby till I hear from you again.

E.P.Landers to Susan Landers

Moten and Adaline, I will write some to you too. I got your letter that you sent by Peden. You all had better send me a pocket full of letters by him again. It took me an hour to read them. I would like to see you all the best kind but I will tell you I am under the tight rules of Jeff Davis. I am mighty weak and no account. I don't no whether I will get through the winter or not. Tell little William Henry to make them open the trunk when ever he wants. I sent him 3 cts by Asa Wright. Tell him to shake it at the other little boys and tell them that rich folks will be rich! Moten I want you to move as soon as you can for I will be better satisfied if you was down there. I have bin sick 6 weeks and have bin here 5 weeks today and no money and not well yet and I am afraid that when I do get well I am afraid that being exposed as the poor solgers has to be I am afraid that I will not get through the winter. So I must close for the want of room. It is cold and cloudy now. Write soon. Moten, I wouldn't let your horse go for you will need it but try to sell the mule if it will sell at all. So no more for this time. I could tell you a heap but I can't write much more.

E.P.Landers to Moten and Adaline Hutchins

Richmond,Va
Nov 19,1861
To Mrs. Susan Landers
Dear Madam,

Your son E.P.Landers has been at our home sick for some 5 or 6 weeks and from a remark I heard him make this morning I fear he has written to you for money to pay for his care and that you may sacrifice some property to send him money. I write to assure you that we do not wish you to do any such thing and that we are willing to share the last cent with him rather than he should suffer for any thing or put you to any uneasiness or trouble on his account. Dont sell anything on his account but rest assured that he will not suffer for anything that can be had in this city for money so long as he will stay at our house. He has been very low and though he recovers slowly I think him out of danger and hope in a few days that you may hear of his entire recovery. I was not aware until this morning of his wanting an account of his board or I would have satisfied him that its of no importance. Please to think of him just as you would have attended me. We have had no little pleasure in his company for we find him as much of a gentleman as any person we ever saw. He is no trouble and while I am away he is great company for my wife who really seems to feel like a mother to him . I hope you will not feel uneasy about him nor sell anything to send money as I know very well it would be a sacrifice without half its value. Please write him of our assurance that all is right.

Yours with respect,

William D.Pemberton
No 15 Pearl Street
Richmond,VA
Weston Williams

Richmond, Va
November 21,1861
My Dear Mother,

Having a chance to send a letter by hand, I will write you a few lines to let you know how I am doing. I'm tolerable well though I have had a hard time of it. I hope this will find you all well for health is a great blessing. I will go to camp next week I reckon if nothing happens though I don't know whether I can stand the camp when I go or not. But I can try it. I never got that letter you sent by Asa Wright till yesterday. He took it on to Yorktown. W.T. brought it to me. I have nothing new to write. I would like to know what is the matter of Uncle Ely that he don't come. I am sorry to hear of you being so uneasy about me for it is no use. You wanted to know if I ever felt a cheak of conscience or not. I often think of these things but the old adamance still reigns. Mamma you had better sell your mule if you can get some money for it for I expect your corn will be very low. If I could tell you all about it you need not to talk about hard times at home for I never saw none till I became a solger. I will write you again when I go to camp, so I have nothing more except to let us try to reconcile ourselves to our lot in this world. Your picture is a great consolation to me. Don't be uneasy about me. If I can't stand camp and don't die, I will come home soon. So goodbye for this time. Excuse this short letter.

E.P.Landers to Susan Landers

Richmond, Va
November 21 1861
Dear Caroline,

I will write some to you but I don't know what to write because I have nothing new to write. Car I would like to be with you a while to tell and hear all the news. I could tell a heap and hear a help but if we never see each other no more let us not forget the happy days that is past by and gone and never cut the twine of brotherly and sisterly affection. I am doing tolerable well. I expect to go to Yorktown in a few days, there to live or to die and I don't want you all to be so uneasy. I am resolved to try it again.If these folks charges me full price I will owe them 28 dollars and that will be right hard to pay. Give my best love and respects to all the girls that seems to feel interested in my sickness. Tell them that I am getting well again. Tell Mat Mc and Ellen N. that they kissed my features for it is like me when I had it taken. They all said that it couldn't be me but tell them if they never see no more of me than that to not forget me. I am the only one of the company that is in Richmond. Only W.T. and he will start tomorrow. I wish I could come with him. Give my love to Harriet and Dan's family. Tell Harriet that I am much obliged to her for her coverlid if I ever get it. Tell her that I will be the best fellow I can. Tell Liz that I have not forgot her yet. Give my love to her and the children. Car I don't know what else to write. I am writing by a lamp light. Give my respects to all inquiring friends and to all who turns to help you. Tell Jim Cruse that Dave is well. Arch and Lige too, so Car don't be uneasy about me. It pesters me to hear of it so nothing more at present only yours affectionately as ever. If I never get there, Home is a sweet word!

E.P.Landers to Caroline Landers

Dear Adaline and Moten,

My dear Brother and Sister, a few lines to you. I had a heap rather read letters than to write them. Ad, if I only could see you all it certainly would be a happy time with me for I want to see William Henry so bad I don't know what to do. I want to see him trotting after the chickens. I hope you can move before

53

Christmas if you can. Moten, I would get shet of my horse for you can work our horses. I don't think that I would like to winter old Bill for nothing for I know that times is hard but need not to talk about hard as long as you can get bread to eat and a good house to stay in and a bed to lie on but if I could only have my health I could make out very well. But I am afraid that I never will have good health no more. I woulda been in camp a week or two ago if I had not taken a relapse but I am coming up again. Moten if you don't mind you will get hurt a braking them steers. I wish I was there to see the fun and Ad will go long to see the fun too. Break them if you can and if you can't, send them to Richmond and you can get 12 and a half cents a pound for them. Tell William Henry he may claim my steer. You must let me know how much corn you are making and how much Mamma has made and how your hogs look, all about it. So nothing more at present as I know of.

E.P.Landers to Moten and Adaline Hutchins

To Brother N.B.,

This morning before breakfast I will write you a few lines. I feel tolerable well this morning hopeing that this will find you and the family well. I have nothing to write but times is hard here in Richmond. Salt is twenty dollars a sack.I expect to quit this place in a few days for I am tired a staying. Pole, W.T. Smith says that somebody stole my brandy the first night. I never even got to smell of it! I'm glad to hear that you are making so much corn. You had better make hogs now out of them shoats. Tell Sarah and little Pole howda for me. You must all do the best you can and I will do the same. I would like to be with you all but you see how it is so I have nothing more to write. So I will close. Write soon and often.

E.P.Landers to N.B. Landers

Richmond, Va
November 1861

This is Sunday morning. W.T. left Richmond yesterday for Georgia and I went down in town and never saw him. Yesterday I aimed to send my letter by him but I did not see him after I got it writ so I will send it any how. I am about well and I will go to camp next week. I feel tolerable well. Mamma I will write again when I get to my company and tell how I seem to stand it. Mamma dont you be uneasy about me for I have found friends here. So far I have got a heap of friends in my company. I think that if I cant stand the campaign and dont die they will send me home but I hope that I will have good health and will be a solger yet but I am a poor solger now. You must do the best you can and I will do the same. I must close now so goodby my good old Mother if I never see you again. I wish I could get home to stay till the weather warms. E.P. Landers to Susan Landers at home

Letter from W.P.Mason to Susan Landers and Caroline Landers written sometime around the end of 1861:

Mamma, I must write you a few lines. Eli is getting well again. I must tell you that Wealthy Landers has sent him a pair of breeches. They are very nice. I went the other day and got them for him. I met up with a heap of my old friends that live in the settlement of Dave's. Dave and family is well and Jim and family is well and [?] and family is well. I was glad to see them. I hant got time to write no more this time. You must look over me so goodby to Susan Landers from WPM.

How do you do Caroline? You must not marry till I do come home. I tell you that the boys is a wanting to come home very bad. They say when they do come home they are agoing to have some powerful good times if you hant all married. You ought to hear them a singing those love songs! It is enough to make you cry to hear them. I want you to write me a big letter and write who is going to see you and write all the news to me. You must excuse me for not writing no more this time. So goodby to Caroline Landers from W.P.Mason.

Letter to Eli and his mother from his cousin, E.M.McDaniel while home on sick leave:
Yorktown, Va Dec.1st 1861
To Mrs. Susan Landers
Dear Sister,

I take the opportunity to write you a few lines to let you know that I am well hoping when these lines come to hand you may read them in improving health. Well Eli, I am in a great hurry for I have a lot of business to attend to today. Eli, I have got mine and Arch's money but he wouldnt pay yours. How come me to get mine I got Sam Dyer and Jim Glover and Tom Peal to help me and me and Arch and Sam Dyer all tried to get yours but he wouldnt pay it because he said that you taken an account of it and he said you might bring it against him again. I told him if you did I would satisfy the account if ever presented and so did Sam and Arch but all that wouldnt do.I told him if he would pay it I would give him a clear re,ceipt and give him double the amount if you ever presented it to him but he said if you would send the account he would settle it. I told him that mayby you didnt have an account of it but he said you did for he saw you set it down on a little memorandum book that you had. Now Eli you send me your account and I will try to get your money for you. Write the amount he got from you and the time he got it and write a gentleman letter. Dont say nothing against him and then if he dont pay it I will give him a good cussing and tell him just what I think of him. Fix it all up just right and in gentleman style. Send it to me just as quick as you can. So no more as I have no news of interest to write. Truly yours.

Cousin E.M. McDaniel to E.P.Landers

1862

Letter to Eli from his cousin, A.W.McDaniel, while he is home on sick leave.

Yorktown,Va
Jan the 1st 1862
Dear Cousin Eli,

      I seat myself at one o'clock to write you a letter before Drill which comes at 4 o'clock to send this by Jim Liddell. I never knew that he was a going till about half an hour ago. I dont know that I can interest you in my letter though I will write a few lines. I am well at present. E.M. is well as to health but he met with the misfortune the other day of burning his hand very bad with burning grease. It is doing very well at this time. We kept it wrapped in dry flour two days and nights then applied a dogwood poultice and it proved good. I have said enough about it as it has been wrote home several times. Dave Cruse is getting better since Pap left. Now I will say that I hope that you may read this in the best of health and find all your folks well and our folks also. You can send this letter over to our house as I cant have time to write them a letter. They are not a going to let none of the privates go home this time so I understand the reason. Some say that it is on account of a Yankee fleet lying off in sight and they are afraid that they will attack us. Now I dont know this to be so but it is reported in camp. I received your letter day before yesterday and was proud to hear from you. You said that you all was not preparing for much fun at Christmas but if there was anything a going that you intended to see it. You ought to been here to a got your Christmas dram and seen all the drunk men and seen them going to the guard tent. Old Cobb give us a dram for Christmas. I hope that you saw a heep of fun with the girls and I hope that you did not forget that my mind was among you all. I hope that you kissed Paulina for me and told her what it was for and if you did not you do it before you leave. Tell her that I have not forgot her loving smiles and purty face. Eli now dont take the start of me because I am not there to take my own part which I dont think you will but dont forget to kiss her and tell her that it was for me. Then you may repeat it again if it suits her but I rather that I was there to do it myself.

      Eli you said that you wanted to know if we had divided our mess or not and wanted to know who was in it and wanted me to save you a place vacant in our tent which we have. We have built two houses for our mess. The Matthews boys,Bob Miner, and Wallis lives in one and us in the other. Dishoney has quit our mess and gone to the Capts mess. Now I will tell you who is in our mess. Me and Lige, Dave Mayfield, and Nute Franklin. Thats 5 and you will make six in one house, 10 and a half by 12 and a half feet. We have got shelves all round our house. Trup Liddleton said that we was very well fixed and looked very nice. He said that it looks like a little nigger quarter. Eli we will see a heap of fun here. I wish that you was with us but I dont want to hurry you back for you had better make good use of your time while you are there for if you ever get back you will know it when you get back. Eli when you come if you can get it, bring some red pepper with you to put in Buck. I reckon that you know what that is. I like to have forgot it.

I bet you and Bill Smith took the leeway with the girls at old Sweetwater. You seemed to talk like that Cobbs Boys was the Boys for the girls and I dont doubt it. If they had of had a sample of them with you they only had the dribble end of them. If they took on so about you dropshot I dont know what they would do if they could get a fare sample. I guess that they would hop round like a cat shot with hot fat. Enough of that!

Excuse this letter. We was mustered in service last night to get our wages. Capt Reeder has got our pay roll and I reckon that we will get our money before many days.

Your cousin until death, A.W. McDaniel

Pap, I hope that you get home safe. Zeb Craig told me that you never got any transportation and that you had to pay your way home. So I hope that you all will not think hard of me for not writing you another letter for I did not have time and you can read this letter. I want some of you to write me a letter for I would like to hear from you. Betsy Ann, Pink is a driving a wagon now. He gets eighteen and a half doilars a month. Thats most twice as much as I get. Give my love to Aunt Pollys folks and tell them to not think hard of me for not writing and for them to write to me. I must close with respects to you and all my friends. Tell them to write.

A.W.McDaniel

Yorktown, Va
Jan.27th 1862
Dear Mother,

All this evening I take pleasure in letting you know that I am at home and feel well as common. This is Monday and I got to Camp last Saturday. I had good luck all the way till I got to Yorktown. But I come out safe. The boat could not land on the York side and we had to land at Gloucester Point. We could not get no place to stay that night and it was very cold and raining and there was no other chance to cross only in a small schooner. We went about 2 miles in a boat about 3 feet across the top. They could not get it to land for the tide was so high. We had to waid about knee deep. I got wet nearly all over and my slip of clothes and letters got wet but none of them was ruined. We went out to the 6th Ga Regiment and stayed all night. Luit Liddle stayed with Luit Culwell and I stayed with Bill Huff. The waves would raise the schooner high as my head and all appearances of danger showed itself. Luit Liddell was the worst scared man you ever saw. But it did not frighten me much for I just thought if we ever got to land we would be on the other side and if the waves wrapped us up I would not be by myself. I was afraid that it would make me sick but I feel no symptoms of it yet. Me and Liddell marched out next morning to camp about 3 miles through mud shoe mouth deep. We got to camp about 9:00. The boys was the gladdest set of boys you ever saw. I have not got through talking yet nor won't in two weeks!

It came my turn to stand guard the next day but I begged off though the next time I will have to stand to the Trug pen. We don't have no picket guard now at this camp. There is some of our boys thats gone down cross Bethel to work on a fort. Ten boys out of every company went. All the boys is well and hearty. They are as fat as pigs. They have eat so much beef till they favor a cow! They throwed away enough beef the other day to make a good milk cow. Enough of such fun.

W.D.Cruse is gone home. I never got to see him. Tell him that he missed his cakes by going home. I took them safe and me and Lige and A.W. and Nute Franklin ate them. Mamma don't be uneasy about me for we are well fixed for living with a good log cabin dobbed as tight as a tater house. We are fixed just as comfortable when we ain't on duty as if we was at home. We have got a straw bed and plenty of blankets. I lay as comfortable as I ought to. I have been out cutting wood today. That is all the duty that I have done. I left the mountains at 9:00 on Monday night and ate my supper at "my old home" on Wednesday night. They was greatly surprised when I stepped in. The old folks applauded as glad to see me as if I had been their son. Mr. and Mrs. Williamson and Emma was still there till Friday morning. Next day I went down to see Cate. They was upstairs but I was met at the door with a kiss. Tell W.T. Smith that Cate looks as well as ever. She read his letter with pleasure. There was two neighbor girls in that evening to wit, Miss Liza Bie and her sister. I went home with Miss Liza and another fellow went with the other. Tell Liz that I've got the Richmond girls hearts! They all have great sympathy for the 16th Ga Regiment and especially for the Flint Hill Grays. They say we are the best soldiers in service. The boys is now drawing lasses and they keep such a fuss about it till I can't write. I found all my things straight at home at the camp. Mr. Pemberton said that he would answer your letter soon. He read my letter a few days before I got there, though they had not read it at the hospital. But there was nothing wrong though I was halted in Richmond and had to show my pass. But then I made the men show me their authority. I enjoyed myself well on the way and also when I got to Richmond. I just felt like I had got back home. Samp Garner stayed with me in Richmond. He said the Pembertons are the best people he ever saw. I got to camp with 4 dollars and 50 cents and left 10 dollars with Mr. Pemberton. We will draw again in a few days. Mamma I hain't got time to write to all as it is time to get supper, but they must all consider themselves included with my best respects and wishes to them. Tell Maryanne that I have not told her pa yet. Tell Charles and William Henry to write. Mamma I have no war news to tell. We are not expecting a fight at this time. There is talk of peace but sorry to say that I can't believe it. I have not had time to before and now my mind is not for writing. We have drawed flour and pork and molasses. We will live well till it is gone. The boys can look very nice now. I will tell you the truth we are well fixed. Give my love to all, not one but all. Tell J.W. Shamblee I never saw Nicholas,but Liddell did. He is not very bad off. A.W. and E.M. is well. They said that they had been wanting to come home sometime. W.P.Mason is well but he has a hard time. He will come this spring. Mamma excuse this letter for I can't think of nothing to write.

E.P.Landers to Susan Landers
Excuse me for I am being pestered

Yorktown, Va
Feb 3rd 1862
Dear Moten and Ad,

I will write you a few lines for fear you will think I am partial,but please don't think so for it is not the case. Well, for fear you never got my other letter I will tell you of my difficulty at Yorktown. On account of the tide and other vessels being anchored at the wharf we could not land our boat on the York side of the river and had to land at Gloucester Point. It was raining and as cold as fury and the tide was very high indeed and I couldn't get a place to stay at that night and no other chance to cross, only on a small schooner about three feet across the top. There were nine of us crossed in it and some of the waves were as high as my head. I got all of my things wet with the waves dashing over in the boat. We went about two miles in it and I waded about knee deep to get into it. It was dark by the time I got to York. I stayed that night with Billy Huff in the 6th Ga Regiment. It has quit snowing now and it is now sleeting like rips. Tell William Henry and Charles and little Pole they mustn't catch a cold if it snows in Georgia. Give my respects to Harriet and their families. I wish I could write to all of them but I haven't got time. The sleet is falling through on my paper so I must quit. I want you to write when you can. So I will bid you farewell.

To Moten and Adaline Hutchins and William Henry from E.P.Landers

Dear N.B. and Sarah,

I did aim to write this side to you, but the sleet is falling through on my paper so bad I can't write. But I hope these few words will satisfy you, for I'll write them with as good feelings as if the whole letter had been to you. I want you to write how you are getting along at the new place and all the other news. Please accept these few words for they are wrote with the best of feelings as a brother. Luit Cain will start directly to old Georgia and I must quit. Excuse this and write soon. Mamma I have said nothing to you in this letter but I hope you will excuse me and consider yourself included.

E.P.Landers to N.B.and Sarah Landers

Yorktown, Va
Feb 3rd 1862
Dear Caroline,

Well H.C. as I have the chance of sending a letter by Luit Cain I will write you a few lines in a great hurry.This leaves me well and I hope that this may find you all well. I wrote you all a letter the other day sent by Capt. Hutchins. It is now a snowing as purty as you ever saw. We have a prospect for a heavy snow but we are comfortable in our cabins with a good fire. Tomorrow I have to stand guard. I have stood guard once since I got back but it never hurt me. I have enjoyed very good health since I left home though A.W.is not well. He has got the yellow jaundice. Well H.C. I've no reliable news about the war to report. It is reported that there were several vessels of war landed at Old Point not far from here. This is sport, but orders came in the other evening to hold ourselves in readiness for a march and we fixed up our guns in order and are now ready at any minute to take the trip. Well all I have to say is just let them come-along and then they will know how they get along.

Well Car you and all the rest of our folks must not think hard of me for not writing to you all individually for I don't have the time for this work to do another thing. Paper is very scarce too. If I fail writing to your satisfaction, it will not be for the want of respects to you. And if anything turns up uncommon you shall hear of it so don't you and the rest of them not think I don't think enough of them to write for if you do you will be mistaken.

Well I had the best of luck all the way through till I got to Yorktown. The wheels rolled me off from the mountain Monday night at 9:00 and they rolled up to Richmond Wednesday evening at 6:00 That was leaving you all tolerable fast! Everything looked so natural. I felt like I had gotten back home and my folks were all very glad to see me. Next morning I went down to see Miss Kate. I was met at the door with great applause and a sweet kiss. They had a lady to see them and when she found out I belonged to the 16th Ga Regiment it was alright. We wear the respected brown of the citizens of Richmond. They say that they believe we will maintain our position at any and all hazards. Caroline I want you to write all the news that you think would interest me. Give my respects to Miss Margaret and Julie H. and the Matt and Vina Ellen and to Miss Paulina. Especially tell her that I sent her a letter by Capt. Hutchins so I will close with my love to you as a brother. Give my entire love to Mamma. Tell her I sent her a letter the other day.

E.P.Landers to Caroline Landers

February 1862
To all my Brothers and Sisters in Gwinnett, one and all,　.

I will write a few lines in great haste. I feel this morning like one alone. I had to cook my breakfast and set down and eat it by myself for all my mess was sick. It made me feel odd. I have been in fine spirits all the time till this morning but the gloomy prospect that hangs over our heads has rather trimmed my feathers. But not withstanding all those gloomy clouds arise I cant help but believe that there is a day ahead that some of us will send the echo of our voice into the valleys of old Georgia in Triumphs of the Liberty and Independence and that we may live in peace once more but there is no telling when that day will come for no one knows how long this war will last. But it is as I said, just so long as the Enemy follows us and persecutes us. General Cobb come in camp the other day and at night he was serenaded with the band of music and he give us an eloquent speech. He said that it was not his will that he was appointed General for he said that he made up his Regiment to live and die with them if needful. He boasted on the 16th Georgia very much and he says in Georgia and on the railroad and everywhere we have been camped we have got the name of good behavior.

Well I cant help writing about the sick for here is E.M. and Nute and Mayfield all three laying here side by side and it is hard to tell which is the worst off and I dont feel well myself but dont let this trouble or bother you for we will do the best we can and that is all any of you can do. So I want you all to write and let me know something about the affairs in Georgia and let me know if the two Dan Liddells and W.R. Miner and Dan McDaniel is going to the war or not. Tell them to come to this company. W.P.Mason is well and has gone to Jamestown after a wagon. It is about 50 miles from here. Well, we are looking for a fight now there is 50 thousand Yanks close by but we dont care for them. General Cobb said the other night that we would be in a fight before long. You must give my love to all the inquiring girls.

I wish I could see William Henry and Charles and Maryann and little "Pole". Charles, if you can walk good you must tell me. William Henry, if you can talk good you must tell me. This is a sorry letter but you see how it is. So goodby for a while.

E.P.Landers to you all

My Friends, let me only ask one kind thing of you
Let it be an easy task Sometimes to think of me!

Yorktown, Va
Feb 20th 1862
To the Connections in general,

Dear Friends,Mother,Brothers, and Sisters, this afternoon I take pleasure in writing to you though it seems like a difficult matter for me to hear from you though Miss Paulina said in her letter that you was all well.That gives me great pleasure. This leaves me well and it is my earnest desire for it to find you all in the same fix. I have enjoyed good health ever since I left home. Well, I don't know what to write first for we are very badly confused at this time on account of the War matters. We are now ready and looking every hour for orders to leave. We received orders day before yesterday to cook four days rations and be ready to march. The wagons was sent off to York after crackers. We had no flour hardly but got plenty of sea crackers. We are expecting an attack every hour. The Yankeys is trying to flank us on water by sending a force up the York and James Rivers and get in the rear of our army and if they try it with a sufficient force they may succeed but they need not to try it with less than 50 thousand men for we are well fortified all over the Peninsular. We have got hundres of acres of land cut down between here and the Yankeys to blockade the way with trees so that they can't come on us with their artillery and it is most impossible for them to advance far by land. Well we receive bad nuse most everyday lately. I suppose you have all heard of the fight at Roanoak Island, North Carolina. The enemy is now in possession of it. They killed many of our men and took 2000 prisoners. McMullins Regt,the one that you all saw pass Mr. McGinnis is all taken prisoners but 3 companies. The Independent Blues is all in prison. They was taken at the Island fight. It is reported that they are now at Fortress Monroe about 20 miles from us but poor fellows we can't help them for all we are close by them. All our boys seems to sympathize a great deal for them but we see how it is. The Yankeys is getting the ends on us most everywhere they attack us. The dispatch of yesterday says that they have taken Fort Donelson in Tennessee and taken a great many of our men prisoners and that the citizens of Nashville had surrendered to Yankeys but I hope to God it aint the truth for if it is you may all look soon in Georgia for they will then have the main railroad and can run their forces both East and West. If this report be true the Drafted Boys will have their hands full. I say Drafted Boys but I only speak in a joke but I understand that there is to be a draft served in Georgia the 4th of March and it grieves me to think that such a thing has to be done for perhaps the draft will fall on some good fellow that woulda been in the army long ago if they could a been spared from home. But if it has to be done I hope that some of them stout able men who has nothing to keep them at home will have to shoulder their guns and walk out in defense of their country in time of need for they are no better than we are that has come out and volunteered for the War. I am proud to think that me and most all my associates formed the resolution to not be forced to the rescue of our country but I hope that those men that is drafted may come with the great resolutions within their hearts to say Victory or Death. I will tell you that is the only way that we ever can succeed. There was a great talk of peace when I first got to Camp but oh to our sorrow we now see it was entirely a mistake. But there is one thing certain. We will hold them uneasy a long time before we will give it up. We will yield to none of their propositions without they be moved on our own terms. We will yield to death first. All our disasters do not seem to discourage our boys much. It seems to put a spirit of fight in them and I hope it will ever reign in them. We need not to think to end such a war as this without some disastrous defeat for we need not to expect to always succeed but I hope in the long run that we may have peace and harmony again and that we once more have the pleasure of tramping over the old hills that we have so often roamed and not only that but to have the pleasure of our friends and relations as an Independent and Free people!

Well now Moten, I would like to say something to you if I knew what to say. If you have to go to War I would like for you to be with us but I don't know what is best and so you must be your own judge for the best is bad enough. Well I will tell you something about my affairs. I reckon that some of the boys will draw money in a few days but I can't draw none this time, me nor Samp Garner neither for we was not present when they was mustered in to get it and there was no requisition made for it but I reckon that I can make out without it but I hant got but 1 dollar 50 cts but there is some owing to me and if I get out I can borry as much as I want but I don't have much use for money only to pay for postage. I reckon that it will be good when it does come for it has been a long enough time a coming. Well now in the close of my letter let me ask you in a kind manner to write soon for I want to hear from you all. Tell all the nuse about the boys and girls and how you have arranged your affairs. If Moten has to leave I don't want Pole to move for it wont do for no man person to be there. Well my dear friends this may be the last time that I ever will have the pleasure of addressing you for times is very uncertain now but if it is, please recollect that this your affectionate son and brother that is speaking to you but I hope that I will never be deprived of writing you for nothing gives me more pleasure than to write to you and to hear from you but let this not discourage us but let us endeavor to surmount all those gloomy scenes and show to the World that we are an Independent Nation!

E.P. Landers to You All

Suffolk, Va. Camp Aner
March 12, 1862
My Dear Mother,

As W.T. is going to send a letter I will write a few lines. This leaves me well except for a bad cold but that is nothing more than I expected after so much exposure. Well I don't know what to write for I have not got time to write nothing hardly. We have moved from the Peninsula and I am not sorry of it but I fear that this will be a good deal of sickness on account of being so badly exposed getting here. There is a good many sick now. E.M. McDaniel is very unwell today and yesterday he was very bad off but is some better today. I put a blister on his breast this morning and give him some powder. He is better now. Cousin A.W. is getting well. He is at Williamsburg. W.T. saw him the other day. He gets the best of treatment there. Well I must hasten through for the mail is nearly ready to leave. Well I reckon that the boys will draw money today or tomorrow, but I will not draw none this time for I was not present when they was mustered in for it and there was no requisition made for it this time but I will only get the money when it comes. If I need any I can borrow as much as I want but I think that I can do on very little. I wrote you a letter the day before we left the old camp but I will not write no more till I get some paper for this is the last that I have got and no chance to get more. You must tell the girls to not think hard of me for not writing for we can't write without we have paper to write on. You must write soon and write all the news for I would like to hear from Georgia very much. Tell W.D. that we wrote him a letter the other day. Luit Cain is now up in Suffolk sick with the pleurisy. I saw Steve the other day. He is in the 1st S.C. Regiment. He is a nice young man and I saw John King the other day. He is first Sergeant of his company. It need not surprise you to hear of us being in Georgia some of these days but I don't know no more than you do. When you write, direct it to Suffolk, Va. Tell Uncle Eli that I will do all I can for E.M. Tell W.T.S. that I have written him one letter and would like to hear from him. Give my best love to all the family. So I will close with my love to you as an affectionate son.

E.P.Landers to Susan Landers

Camp Anners Suffolk,Va
March 15th 1862
My dear Mother

I this morning take pleasure in writing you a few lines to let you know how we are getting on. As for myself I cant tell the truth and say that I am well but I think that it is the cold and being exposed to the weather and broke of my rest waiting on the rest of the sick. I am sorry to tell such news to you but I reckon I had better tell the truth. All of my mess is down sick but me that is all that is in our tent. E.M. McDaniel has been very bad off for several days but I think he is some better this morning. W.N. Franklin had a hard chill this morning and is now bad off and also W.M. Mayfield had a chill this morning and is now very sick and A.W. has not come from the Hospital. He is in Williamsburg though I heard from him. He is improving so that takes all in my tent. There is a great deal of sickness in camp now but no more than I expected for we was the worst exposed of any set of men I ever saw but I hope that I will stay up to wait on the rest of them for they are not able to wait on each other but I fear that I will fail for I can hardly keep up now and have to be up and down all night. If I have to wait on them and drill too I think that they aught to excuse me from all other duty but they will not do it. But I will do the best I can for them but the best is bad enough for we are right where there is no accommodation to be found. They are in the tent lying on the ground but that is solgers fare anyhow. Well you may tell Uncle Eli's folks that there is nothing that I can do for E.M. that will be too good for him for I will try to lend a hand to him as a brother solger. The boy is in a great trouble and is very restless. The boys has all just drawed their money 2 months wages but I will not draw any this time but I have drawed Nute's and E.M.'s and Mayfields. I hold 54 dollars now for E.M. and I reckon that I will collect some more of his debts this evening. Tell James Cruse that I will try to collect that Dyer note for E.M. though S.E. Dyer is not here. I don't know whether the Capt will draw his or not. He was left at the old camp to guard what was left. He is not well. I have not heard from Mr. Pemberton yet. I dont know what to think of the old fellow. I reckon that I can get enough money to make out on but I havent got but one dollar in the world but that dont make much difference for we dont need much only to get paper and stamps but that takes a right smart for I give 25 cts for 3 sheets of this paper and was glad to get it at that. Well I cant write as I wish to for the poor boys is moaning with their pain so bitterly that it has confused my mind till I cant compose it but you need not to expect to derive much pleasure from this letter for there is no good news in it. We are expecting to leave here in a short time and if we do I dont know what in the world we will do with the sick for there is no hospital in Suffolk. But I reckon if we do leave they will be sent to Petersburg. Mamma I have saw a good many of my old acquaintances since I come to this place. We heard that the Independednt Blues was taken prisoners but it is a mistake for I have saw several of them, the Michel boys and Rich Martin and several others. They say they have never saw a Yankey. You aught to see the boys raking for what each other owes. Well you must give my best love to all the family. I wish I had time to write more but I tell you I am kept busy. You must write soon and let me know how you are getting on with your business and all the news. You must try and do the best you can for there is no telling how long I will be separated from you but I know one thing. It will be just as long as the Enemy follows and persecutes us for it never shall be said that I returned home with the Enemy pursuing in my tracks. You must tell my friends to not think hard of me for not writing for the truth is I hant got the chance. I am now due 4 letters in Georgia and hant got time nor paper to pay them. Give my entire respects to Miss P.H. Tell N.B. to write. It is now raining and a prospect for a wet spell and if there is one surely some of our sick will die. It looks hard that men should suffer so on account of the infamous Yankeys. You see how it is so good by My Dear Mother.

E.P.Landers to Susan Landers

Weldon, NC
March 23rd 1862
My Dear Mother,

It has been a pleasure to me to write you a few lines in order to let you no my condition. I am tolerable well. This morning we're now on our way to Goldsborough, NC. We left Suffolk yesterday and got to this place last night. We will stay hear tell this evening. We met Asa Wright hear last night. He was on his way to Suffolk. It is about 100 and 50 miles from Suffolk to the place that we are going. I have just read your letter and all was right in it. I was setting on the platform when I read it. I just turned around and is now riting on the place where I was setting. I'm glad of that money you sent but now I wish you had it back for I could dun without it for wheh I left Suffolk I got 4 dollars from A.W. and all of my mess is left in Suffolk but me. That is all in my tent. E.M. and Nute and Mayfield is down sick though I reckon that you have heard it for I wrote Uncle Eli a letter the other day. At that time we did not think that E.M. would live but when we left yesterday he was a great deal better. I think now by good attention he will soon get well. A.W. come from the hospital the next evening after I wrote Uncle Eli's letter. He is well and was left with E.M., Nute, and Mayfield. He's very bad off but is getting better. Well you heard a false tale about me starting to a battle and giving out. It is very true I did not get to the battle but I got as far as any of the rest did. We thought we was going into a fight but the enemy did not come out to face the music. They say that they are fighting at the place we are going to. I wouldn't be surprised if we don't get to try it before many days and I won't care if we do but it makes me feel bad to think that out of my mess I am all that is able to carry arms but I will try to do my fighting and some for them too. I reckon we will be stationed at Kinston, NC but I don't know how long we will stay there. We will be 100 and 50 miles nearer home than we was at Yorktown. I haven't got time to write much. The train is nearly ready to start and I want to mail my letter before I start but if I had time I could write the bulliest letter ever you read from me for my heart is full. If I only could reveal it. I have got the worst cold I ever had and now am exposed and will be for several days. Sometimes we are gone from camp 2 or 3 days without a tent to lie in and very often in the snow or rain. But I hope that the strong arm of protection will be with me through all of my trials. Give my love to all the friends. Capt and Luit Cain was left in Suffolk sick though I think they will be on in a few days. So without I could write a full letter I will close with my best wishes to you all and to our Country. The folks must not think hard of me for not writing for the truth is I don't have the chance to write since we left Yorktown. But my silence don't stop my respects to all my friends. I have writ this in great haste so goodby my dear old Mother if I never see you again. I will write soon as we get stationed.

E.P.Landers to Susan Landers

Goldsboro, NC
March 25th 1862
My Dear Mother,

   I am again permitted to drop you a few lines which is a great pleasure to me. These lines leaves me well and I hope that they may find you well. I wrote you a letter last Sunday while we was at Weldon, NC and I promised you that I would write again when we got stationed. We are 4 miles from Goldsboro, NC. We got here the 24th of the month. Well I don't no what to write first for I have no good news to relate more than we are about 300 miles nearer home than we was at Yorktown though we are 500 miles from home yet. There is a great number of soldiers round here now. We are expecting a general engagement now every day. The enemy is about 60,000 strong and are advancing on Goldsboro while our number is about 40,000. But we are reinforcing our army every day. We got orders to hold ourselves in readiness to be ready at any minute. No person is allowed to leave the camp only to the spring and back but there is no telling what will be the result. But if the enemy still keeps advancing the result will be blood no doubt. The enemy is in possession of New Bern and are now 8 miles toward Goldsboro and if they should succeed in getting this place they will soon ruin North Carolina. But we feel assured that we have the boys now who will stand the test and by so doing I hope that we may badly defeat them in their attempt.

I wrote to N.B. in my last letter just what I thought was best about coming for I know enough about it to no that he can't stand it and now I again tell him as one that wishes him well to stay at home and make corn and he will be of some service to his folks and to himself and to his country and if he turns out to the hardships of a company he will soon quit serving in this world! But as I said before if he will go I want him to come to this company. I understand that there is a call for 160 more men from Gwinnett which I am sorry to hear of for I don't know what you will all do for it looks like that's nearly all of the men that will have to go. But you must all do the best you can for there is no telling when I will be with you in the fields again. But I will try to do all I can here when we draw money I will try to send you some 30 or 35 dollars. I think that I can pay my debts and then spare that much but I don't know when we will draw. We have a heap of sickness in our Regt. Now there is about 150 men left in Suffolk sick, 15 from our company. I understand that 10 of our regiment has died there but none of our company. E.M. is getting better. W.N. Franklin is too. There is several sick at this camp. Nathaniel Russell is lieing very low. This is what I hate to have to tell. We had to witness the death of one of our worthiest solgers last night to wit, William Dickison. He died at 4 o'clock. We all mourn the loss of him very much but there is one thing that I am glad to say. He died in Triumph of Honor. Throughout the company he will ever bear the name of a worthy solger. I don't think he had an enemy in the company but poor fellow has passed through into a world unknown to mortality as many others has and may soon well follow. But I hope that if I be one that I will depart with honor to my Soul and Body as a good solger. It makes me feel bad to see so many of of our men dieing. It looks like that our Regiment has had hard luck but we have no reason to wonder. I want you to write soon and write all the news. I would send you some stamps but the rules is so tight that I can't get to town and I can't buy none in camp. I have got some but I had better keep them. W.P.Mason is gone somewhere after a wagon but I don't know where. He left while we was at Suffolk and I've not seen him since. We will send William's corpse home by a man by the name of Odom that was here to see Andy and Henry Odom. W.M. Massey has been sick but is now getting better. Give my love to all the family. I will close for I hant got time to write much for we have to drill so much. We have to go on a Brigade Drill now directly. Tell W.D. that he don't no nothing about hard times! Tell him I will write him if I get the time. He had better stay home till he gets well. There is not much of interest in this letter but you must make the best of it as you can and write soon is my request while I remain your son as ever. So goodby for this time.

E.P.Landers to Susan Landers

Near Yorktown, Va
April 16th 1862
Dear Mother,

In great haste I will write you a few lines this morning to let you know that I am well. Luit Cain will start home this morning on a sick furlough and I thought that I would send you a few lines. I will send you 10 dollars by him. I got it from R.N. Miner. I did not know but what you would need it and I would have no chance to send it. All us boys will send our money with Capt Reeder. It will all go to his house and you can go up there and get it. I will send you more when I draw but I don't know when that will be. I am going to try to get to see John Mathews today. They camped at our old winter quarters. The solgers are coming in as fast as the boats can bring them. There will be 100 and 50 thousand men here by night. I think they are fixing for it now every day but I can't tell when it will be. It may be before night and it may not be in a week. Mamma I just wrote this to let you know about that money. I hadn't took the notion to send it when I wrote Ads letter and I hant paid Mr.Pemberton yet and if you get in a place that you need my money you may have it for he is able to do well without it. Mamma my best wishes will be with you all and all that I can do for you I will do with pleasure. I heard from E.M. last night. He is doing very well. We heard that Mose Herrington was dead. He was left at Suffolk. Dave McGinnis is in Goldsboro sick and very bad off so nothing more at this time as I wrote yesterday. You must do the best you can and write soon. I sent you a dollars worth of stamps too. Let me know if you get them.

E.P.Landers to Susan Landers

Yorktown, Va
April 23rd 1862
My Dearest Mother,

I am again permitted to answer another letter from you which came to hand yesterday which gave me great pleasure to hear you was all well for that is a little more than I can say for myself at present. I have been rather puny for several days but I have not been past doing duty but if I don't get better I will have to report to the doctor,. But I reckon that it is the cold that's the matter with me being so exposed to the weather and broke of my rest for we ain't got to sleep but two nights since the 16th, the day of the fight.

Now I am going to tell something about the fight because I know that there will be so many different descriptions given. I hate to say anything about it but I aim to tell the truth if I can. Well on the 16th about 3:00 in the evening, the enemy made their attack and run into our pickets. We was about half a mile from the line when the firing commenced. We all went in double quick to the rescue of our brothers and when we got there the enemy was nearly to our breastworks, in fact they had part of them in possession and we run in an open fire on them. We did not have time to organize our regiment. We just run in and shot when we had the chance and never formed no line. If a man could get behind a tree it was alright. Some of the boys never fired a gun. Some lay behind logs as close to the ground as young rabbits till the battle was over. One or two of our company run back to camp but as for my part I thought I would stay till the fun was over. There was the 7th, 8th, 11th, and 16th Georgia Regiments engaged in the fight, along with the 5th North Carolina and a Louisiana regiment. The Yankees made the North Carolina regiment retreat from their own breastworks and the Yanks took it but in come our 7th Georgia brothers and their colonel who immediately ordered a charge and the brave boys obeyed the command with the greatest applause and hollering and retook the battery without the loss of a man with only one or two wounded. The fight lasted till about dark when the enemy retired. Our boys killed and wounded about eighty but we don't know the exact number. We fought mostly across a pond that Jim Magruder had made on a small creek. But the brave rascals made a charge through the pond on us but there was but few of them that lived to get back to the side where they started. There was only two of our regiment killed and six or seven wounded. Old Mr. Gassaway was killed dead and one of Captain Skelton's men was killed. I was standing in three feet of him when he was shot. Me and him was shooting from behind the same tree. I think the old fellow killed two of them before they got him. Me and him was before any of our company. We saw in about seventy five yards of them and I took two fair pops at them from that tree but there was so much smoke I could not see whether I killed anyone or not but I don't know what is the reason for I took deliberate aim at them! The old man was shot right in the forehead but it did not frighten me as bad as I expected it would but I tell you when the bullets would whistle around my head I felt sort of ticklish. But I thought that there was no use in standing back. If I got killed I couldn't help it but as the good Father would have it, I came out without a scratch. That was on the 16th and we had to stand picket till the 20th without any relief and I tell you it has most outdone me. We will have to go out again tomorrow. We haven't had no attack since the 16th. Only the other night there was a few of them running into our pickets but they didn't follow them back to our regiment. The pickets was afraid to go out anymore. I must close for now with best wishes to you all.

E.P.Landers to Susan Landers

Yorktown, Va
April 25th 1862
Dear Mother,

I will write only a few lines though I hant got time to write much. This leaves me well as to health but I feel very much wearied as I have just come off of picket duty. As for nuse I have a good deal but not much that is reliable. We have not had no fighting since the 16th only some skirmishing with our pickets but not much damage done on either side. This morning we had some heavy skirmishing but none killed on our side but one was wounded in the face. We are expecting another fight every day but I can't tell nothing about it. I wrote you a letter the other day and gave you the details of the battle as near as I could. William Wallis come to see~us the other day. He will start home in the morning or back to Petersburg where his brother John is in the hospital. I will send this letter by him and I will send you 5 dollars by him. I would send you more but we have not received pay yet and I hant got but 8 dollars by me at this time. I sent you 10 dollars by Luit Cain. I borrowed it from R.N. Miner. We will draw pay when this excitement gets over. The quartermaster has got the money for us now but don't want to pay it over till the fight is over and I think it is a very good idea for we might get killed and lose it. Well Mammy I don't know what to write that will interest you for my mind is confused so I can't compose it but if I fail to tell the nuse by writing you will have guessed at the rest. But I have been in service nearly 9 months and I have never saw such times as we have now for a man is in danger of his life to leave the camp and the orders that was give to pickets that relieved us this morning was that if any man run or give orders to run without orders from the Commanding Officer, he is to be shot! There was a large force come on us this morning and I tell you the bullets sung round our heads like mad bees but they soon retired and the firing is now ceased. Mammy when we draw I will send you some more money if nothing happens. I understand that Mr. Pemberton has moved out in the country one and a half miles. Nick Shamblee told me. I will pay him if I get the chance to send it by hand. If you can, I would be glad if you will send me a wool hat by the first one that passes. And another thing, I know it will be a hard matter to get but if you can send me an oil cloth for we hant got no tents and so much wet weather that I need it. But don't put yourself to too much trouble nor pay 2 prices for it for I had rather do without it than for you to do so. N.B., I received your letter and was truly glad to hear from you. You told me to do my best at the Yanks. You needn't to doubt but what I looked low down in the sights at them and I think that I injured two of them. I would write you a full letter if I had paper but you must read this in answer to it as my best respects goes with it to you and your family.

Mammy you must write when you can and tell Moten and Ad to write. Give my best love to them and Harriet and to all the connections and inquiring friends. Tell Liz that W.P. has not come from the hospital yet. I don't know how he is. Give my best respects to all the girls for I will have to quit writing till I can get to where I can get some paper. Paper and tobacco are two things that can hardly be found in this country. At the present we are camped in 300 yards of John Martin and all the boys. John Matthews looks the best I ever saw him. There is about 30 Regiments of Georgians here now. We miss old man Gassaway mightly but the poor old fellow is lying over here in the woods and his brains is scattered over the ground. I was in 3 feet of him when he got killed. As Bill Dyer says, some of the boys leaped to the rear but I will mention no names and tell no tales out of school! I must close for I hant got time to write much. Be careful with my mare and don't make a fool of her. Tell W.D. I wish he was here to see the fun but he had better not come till he gets well. So I will close with my best wishes to you all as a son and brother.

E.P.Landers to You All

April 1862
Dear Mother,

A few lines to you as I dont know when I will have the chance to write again. I am well today and I hope this will find you all well. You must read

E.M.'s letter to get the news for I hant got time to write it to you both. I merely write this because I did not have time to send another one by Mr. Shamblee. I sent you 45 dollars by him. I told you I wanted you to pay Mrs. Reeder 13 dollars for me. I want you to pay her and get a receipt from her in my name. I said in my letter that there was no prospect for a fight here and the next morning the Ball opened and we have had some of the beautifulest Fighting that we ever have had! It is the greatest victory of all the War according to the number that was engaged. Cobbs Brigade has done the work at last! It is the first time they ever had a showing and they have showed themselves. I was in the Fight on Thursday but on Saturday I was detailed to cook. It is the first time I have ever been out. I think we will try it again soon and I tell you I dread it. Of all the fighhts I've ever been in I never had such feelings as I had on Thursday and I hope I never will have again. A good many of our reglment was wounded that day and several killed.

I want you to write soon. My Dear Mother if I never meet you again and should meet the dread fate of some of my friends I hope to meet you in a world of peace and pleasure. There is so many dangers staring me in the face I feel the need of a strong Protector.

I sent you some needles by Mr. Shamblee. I merely sent them for Compliments. Give my love to all the Family. Excuse these few lines. I will send it in E.M.'s letter so I will quit.

E.P.Landers to Susan Landers

Letter to Susan Landers from her son-in-law, W.P. Mason:

General Hospital, Petersburg, Va
May 14 1862
To you all. I hant got time to write you all a separate letter so I will write a little to you all:
Dear Mother,

I seat myself this evening to drop you a few lines from which you may learn I received those lines from you. I was more than glad to hear from you and to hear you all was well. Your letter found me unwell but I hope that I will get well again soon. I went this morning in the doctor's office to talk with him. He said that I had the rheumatism in my legs. He said that was the cause of them a hurting me so he said it was from cold and exposure. It did commence in my shin bones just above my ankle and now it has got up in my knees. I dont know what I will do. I dont have no chance to bathe them here. I have a great mind to go back to the regiment. I think that I will be able for duty in a month. Mammy I want to see you and Caroline in the worst sort a way. I am in hopes that I will get to come and see you before long. I think of you often. I hant forgot you all even if I am a long ways off. I am about 6 hundred miles from you now and the Yankeys is in 10 miles of me. There is such a chat a them trying to take this place but I dont think they will myself. I must close.

from W.P.Mason to Susan Landers

Moten, I will drop you and Adaline a few lines. You can see on the other side how I am. I hope when those few lines come to hand they will find you all well and doing well. Moten, I reckon you are like the rest of the men thinking that your time is but short to stay at home. It is very bad times now. I do wish the war would stop. There is a heap of pore souls a dying besides what is getting killed on the battlefield. I dont no precisely how many men has died in our regiment but it is about 150 men. That is awful. Moten, I want you and Add to write to me. I must come to a close for this time.

from W.P.Mason to Moten and Adaline Hutchins

To N.B. Landers and family,
I take my pen in hand to drop you a few lines. I am not well but I mend slowly because of the rheumatism. It gets worse on me. As to nuse I hant got none that is good to write to you. Times is bad here now. Our men just keep a dying. I reckon that you have heard that Dave McGinnis is dead. He died at Goldsborough. I was sorry to hear of his death but we all have to die. N.B. I want you to write to me as soon as you get this.

from W.P.Mason to N.B.Landers and family

[Editor's Note: W.P. "Pink" Mason died in November, 1862.]

Portion of undated letter:

Our men was whipped very bad. Took 800 prisoners killing 1200 but our loss was very heavy. About 500 there was. A NY Regt. hoisted a Confederate flag and hollowed for help and a Florida Regt. went to their assistence taking them to be their friends and when they went as close as the Yankeys wanted them, they began to fire on them, the Floridians finding them to be their enemy. They let in on them and slain nearly everyone of them that was shot. If they get by with such undermining tricks I don't know what we will all do. It looks like they have sot into whip us but maybe its all for the Better. The hotter the war the sooner the peace! I dont see no other chance only for every man to have to go. Moten if you have to go I want you to come to this company with Cain. If you do come dont fetch but one suit of clothes besides what you wear. Mamma dont send me no clothes for I cant take care of them. Send me a good wool hat though by the first one passing for there is no chance to get one here. N.B. there is no use for you to come here for you couldnt stand what we have to undergo a month. W.P. is in Petersburg yet, though he is better. I want to hear from you all mity bad. Give my love to all the Connections and friends. Tell Miss P.H. I received her small letter of about 2 sheets which came yesterday. Give her my best respects. Direct your letters to Bivouac, Va and write soon. I would write all day if I had time but the mail will start in a few minutes. We are lying in an old field not knowing what minute we will leave. I dont know what to tell you for the best you must only do the best you can. My desire is with you. If I never see you again which it looks very doubtful though it is not impossible. Every hospital is full of the sick. So nothng more at this time. A.W.and E.M. is well. R.N. is well too. Tell Cruse not to come if he aint well.

E.P.Landers to Susan Landers

Camp Near Richmond, Va
May 29th 1862
Dear Mother and Lonely Sisters,

I your son and brother takes pleasure in writing to you to let you know that I am yet in the land of the living. But not to say right well. I have got the jaw ache though it don't pain me any today. I hope that this may find you all well and in good health for that is the greatest blessing that we enjoy. It has been some time since I heard from you by letter but I understand that N.B. has gone to the War and I feel very anxious to hear from you to know how you are making out by yourselves. Though I know it is a bad time with you all I think that N.B. has done very wrong in leaving home for he will not be apt to be much service in the army on account of his health while he might a done so much good at home for we all know that we must eat as well as fight and they could not compel him to go. But I reckon that he felt it his duty to go but before 12 months he will wish that he had a took my advice for I begged him in all my last letters to not go and told him how it was and now he has put his head in the halter. He will have to do the best he can but being as he intended to go I had rather than 100 dollars that he had come to this company. I can't hear nothing from Moten whether he is gone or not. I have been very much disatisfied ever since I heard that N.B. was gone for I don't know what you will do for I reckon that Moten will have to go too but you must do the best you can and get shet of some of your stock and don't try to tend too much land. Tend the best spots and you will make more than to try to tend all and if you can't feed her I reckon you will have to sell my mare but I hate mitely to part with her but you must do what you think best for I don't want you to keep her and suffer on account of it. But keep her if you can and if you sell her be very careful who you sell to for these times there is no telling what man or money is good. Ad, you and H.C. must be very careful with the horses and the plow or you will have some old runaway scrapes. You had better tend as much bottom land as you can for that is where the corn grows but I reckon that you know your own business best for you are there where you can see what is needed while I am many miles away but my best desire is with you and for you and under the present conditions of affairs I feel it my duty to send my money to you. I did think that I would finish paying Mr. Pemberton but as he is so very wealthy and you so dependent I think it no more than my duty to let what money I can spare go to help support you. I will say no more about that.

I haven't anything very interesting to write but we have moved since I wrote to you last. We moved off of the River on the other side of Richmond. We are in about 3 miles of Richmond but I can't get no chance to go to see my old friends. We come through Richmond the other day but we was not allowed to stop. There is great fear of the Yankeys taking Richmond. They are in sight of us with a large force. We are expecting a general engagement eery day. It is thought that there will be the hardest fighting around this place that ever has been heard of for the Enemy will do their game fighting to get the city but our men has formed a resolution for the streets to flow with blood before we give it up. There was a fight in hearing of us on the 27th. We could hear their guns plain but we have not heard how it went. I want you to write as soon as you can and tell me all the nuse and if N.B. and Moten is gone. Let me know the number of their regiments and the letter of their company and their P.O. so that I can write to them. Tell them to write to me. Elijah and Arch is both complaining this morning. Pink is in Richmond yet but is getting well. George W. Atkinson is dead. He died on the 26th. He had his health best of arry man in the company till a few days before he died. He took the brain fever. Tell Sq Mc that I saw William Henry yesterday. He is well and in fine spirits. I meet up with more of my old Georgia friends here than if I was in Georgia! Please send me some good strong thread and needles for I have lost mine and send me a hat too. So I will close.

E.P. Landers to Susan Landers

A Camp Near Richmond, Va
June 10th 1862
My Dear Mother and Sisters,

I feel proud that I am permitted to answer another letter from you which came to hand yesterday and as according to your request found me well. This leaves me in good health hoping you may read it in like manner. I have nothing new to write at present but I think that I can afford to reply to all your letters. From the reading of the letters that come to this company I see that it is reported that I was dead but I feel blest and happy to inform you that it is not the case. I have received them things sent by Cain and they come in a good time for I was nearly bareheaded and the next day was a wet day. I see now what a great advantage it is to have friends to provide when a person has no chance to help themselves. But it looks like if you can provide for yourself that I need not be uneasy about myself. It makes~me feel bad when I think how hard you have to struggle for a support in your old days but we all see how it is for we know there is no other chance till the word is given Peace and I fear that will not be soon but oh may the time speedily come when I will have the privilege of enjoying the comforts and pleasure of my old peaceful home where I spent so many days of pleasure and not knowing then how to appreciate it! But that time has passed not to return.

Mr. Liddell came to camp yesterday and I was glad to see him for I knew I would hear from home. Well H.C. you wanted to know what we get to eat. We get meat and bread. Sometimes we get enough and sometimes we don't but we have not suffered bad since we come to Richmond. We don't get hardly any salt though. That is the worst difficulty but on a march we don't get much but this morning we had one of the best messes of bacon dumplings out of jail. We have bought right smart of little extras to eat but had to pay so high for them till our money has give out and we hant drawed any yet nor I don't know when we will. It looks like they never will pay me. I am due over 100 dollars in wages but this is the first time I have ever been without money yet. But I am not by myself for nearly all the company is in the same fix. But we will all do the best we can. We haven't got no tents nor don't want none till winter time. Mamma, you said that you did not think that I ever would read your letter but you must not think that I am killed everytime you hear of a battle. It is true I am just as liable as any person but I have been spared till now. I was close by the fight but was not engaged in it. I could hear them but did not see them. It was a very hard struggle indeed lasting 8 hours of hard fighting. The loss was very heavy on each side. Our loss was about 3000 but greater on the other hand. We drove them off the field taking many prisoners. We don't know when we will try it again. We have moved about 1 mile from the place I wrote before of the picket line to rest. Just one company has to go on picket at a time so we will get to rest.

I don't want you to be so uneasy about me for I will try to do the best I can. Liz I am glad you thought to write to me. I would be glad to reply to it individually but you may consider yourself included in this. Tell the little boys they must quit fighting. I would like to see them take a twist. Tell Margaret I ain't told her Pa yet. Give my entire love and respects to Ad and Harriet and family and to all inquiring friends and especially of the fair ladies of Sweetwater.

Well Mamma I don't know what is best for you to do with my mare for I am afraid that she will be ruined if she is not used some and I won't want to take less than she is worth and I don't know what to say but if you keep her try to get some old sturdy man to plow her a few days but don't let her out all the time. Mamma a few words concerning yourn and Sarahs affairs about living together. You had better live separate. You know it will be best for you both. You must not work too hard for you cant hold out at it. It would be a pleasure to me to run round your young corn patch in the upper bottom but instead of coming towards home there is a great talk of us having to go to Maryland to reinforce General Jackson but we don't know for certain. I told you that I had nothing to write and I reckon you will see its true. Send my respects to Moten and N.B. in your letters. Tell them to let me know who is in their mess. This is a rainy wet day and looks like it will rain all night but me and E.M. and A.W. has got a blanket stretched till it don't leak much so with my best respects to you all I will bring my letter to a close by saying I remain your affectionate son and brother as ever and by requesting you to write when you can hoping that the time will soon come when I will see you again but if you on earth I never see, in all your prayers remember me.

E.P. Landers to his Mother Susan Landers

Mamma, your ambertype is in Petersburg in the Captain's trunk.

Camp Near Richmond, Va
June 21st 1862
My Dear Mother and Sisters,

I this morning seat myself in order to inform you that I am well but feel very drowsy for I have just got up and it is about 2 hours by sun. I hope that you may read this in the best of health. As for news I have none that is interesting only the same old war news and I reckon that you hear enough of that but I believe that is the general talk and study among the people. Now we have not had but very little fighting here since the 3lst but we had had some very heavy skirmishing. One of our regiments attacked the Yankeys the other evening and they fired in like smoke. For a while I thought that we was going to have a general engagement. Our regiment was called in line of battle and all prospects for a fight was shown but the Yankeys run back and our men never followed them. We are looking for another big fight every day but we cant tell when. We are camped in burning distance of each other. We bum each others camp every day. The Yankeys threw a bum in the camp of the 8th Georgia Regiment yesterday and killed one man and wounded 4 others. It is thought that they will die. One of their legs was shot all to pieces and another ones shoulder was shot off. There is some killed or wounded everyday on picket. A man never knows what time he may be shot but we have not lost narry man yet but the 24th Georgia has lost 2 or 3. They was on picket the other day and we sent a scouting party out over the lines to stir up the Yanks and the password was "Stonewall" so if they had to run back that our pickets would know them. One of the pickets saw a man in front of his line and hollowed "Stonewall" to him but it happened to be a Yankey and in the place of giving the password in return he shot him through and says,"Goddam you, that is Stonewall." But another one of our pickets immediately shot the Yank. I guess that he thought he had got Stonewall!

I wrote you a letter 8 or 10 days a~go but I thought I would write again as I had nothing else to do for I am tired doing nothing but we will have to drill 4 hours evry day and I believe that some exercise is best. I don't like this place for a camp. It is a low level place and no good water.We use water out of a little hole dug out in the ground about 3 feet deep and you know that it ain't good but I expect we will have to stay here a good while but I don't care for we are all in for the war anyhow. But I would be glad if I could camp somewhere on Beaver Run but there is so many of the invading scamps round us we must not choose our place to live if we intend to be a free people. We have not drew any money yet but I sold a pair of pants that I did not need for 6 dollars and then I made 5 dollars in a trade so I have got enough to last me a while yet but money is scarce as hen's teeth. In this company everything is so high. We have to pay a dollar and fifty cents a pound for butter and a dollar for a small frying chicken, two dollars a pound for soda, a dollar and fifty cents for a quire of paper and everything else in proportion. I will draw 66 dollars if the rest only draws two months wages.

I would like to hear from you as often as possible but I know you can't write as often as I do but when you do I want you to tell all about your affairs for that is what I want to hear. I want to know how your crop looks and how you hold out to work it and how the hogs looks and everything of that nature and if you get milk a plenty. I think if I was at home I could get a pound of butter for less than a dollar and a half.I often think of the good milk and butter at home that the infernal Yankeys are keeping me away from but if I was all the one I might complain but many others is in the same fix. I have not received a letter from N.B. and Moten yet. I would like very much to hear from them. I don't know how to direct letters to them but R.N.Miner got a letter from Bill the other day and he said that N.B. was well. Well Mamma I have studied a great deal about your condition and about my mare. I don't know what to say about it but I am afraid that she will be ruined not being worked and I don't think that you can feed her so I have concluded if you can get 125 dollars for her that you had better sell her but mind who you sell to for you don't know who is good for thier debts. You must use your own judgment and do the best you can. It grieves me to lie round here in the shade knowing how hard you all have to work at home but those things we can't help. Tell W.D.C. I wrote him a letter on the 18th. John Matthews says remember his respects to you all. He is well. All of them boys is well but Wyley Hopkins. He is gone to the hospital. Give my best love and respects to Harriet and Dan and the children. I would like to see them but I want you all to be included in this letter.

William Henry you must salt my mare and little steers and we will go halves. You and Charles must quit fighting and fight like most little boys, run them behind their mummies and whip them. You must excuse this sorry letter for there is nothing new to write. W.A.W. is well but E.M. is not. He has been lingering for a week but wrote a letter home this morning. W.P. and R.N. is well. I hear the cannons a shooting now. They will keep it up all day but none of their shot don't reach our regiment. Give my best respects to all the connections and to all inquiring friends and receive a good portion for yourself for there remains a good portion in my heart for you. Give my respects to McDaniel. Give him my thanks for his kindness to you. So with my respects to you as a son and well wishes I will close for this time hoping to hear from you soon.

E.P.Landers to Susan Landers

Portion of a letter written by Eli P.Landers from Camp Comfort near Richmond on June 21st, 1862:

My Dear Brothers N.B. and Moten,

I seat myself to write to you a few lines to let you know that I am well hoping that this may find you well also. I have been looking to hear from you sometime. I hant got nothing to write more that we have a little fun here ever once in a while but hant had no hard fighting since the 31st but we have skirmishing everyday. There was a small battle the 18th about 4 miles from here. We lost about 40 men but it's thought that abo~t 100 Yankeys was killed. We are camped in 5 miles of Richmond. Us and the Yankeys are camped in burning distance of each other. They play on one another from their batterues. Our men tossed a few bumbs in the Yankey camp and you never saw men strike tents so fast in your life! But the Yankeys threw a bumb in the camp of the 8th Ga yesterday and killed one man and wounded 4 others. There is some killed or wounded everyday on picket but none of our regiment hant got killed yet but the 24th Ga has lost 2 or 3. They was on picket and sent out a scouting party to stir up the Yankeys and the password was "Stonewall" so if they had to run back our pickets would know them. One picket saw a man and hollered "Stonewall" to him and it was a Yank and in the place of giving the password in return he shot the picket through and says "Goddam you, that is Stonewall." But another picket shot him down. I reckon he thought he had got some of Stonewall! N.B. and Moten I want you to write to me soon and let me know how you stand the camp and how you like the fun and who is in your mess and all about it when you.........

Portion of undated letter:

Mamma if you don't feel able to work I dont want you to do it. What money I send home is for your use and if you dont feel stout enough to work you can hire a little work done to do the hardest work. Anyhow I would not try to tend much land this year though if Add and H.D. keeps well they can tend 8 or 10 acres. I want to know if Mr. Mathews will tend our upper bottom. Give my best respects to him. I've been informed that he is a good friend to you and them is the kind of people that gain my affection. I have studied a great deal about my filly and I cant tell for my life what is best to do for I do hate to part with her and I know she is nothing but an expense but I know I never will get another one that I like as well if I should live to need one. I want to know of N.B. what he will take for his saddle and then let me know. Give my respects to him and to all the family. Tell Harriet and Dan and children to remember me. Give my love to A.W. and E.M. and to all the family and to all inquiring friend. It is getting dark and I must quit. R.N. Miner is well. W.N. Franklin is sick today. Tell A.W. and E. M.to write and I want you to write when you can. Give my respects to G.W. Shamblee. If you know anything H.C. let me know and I will write to him but I have forgotten how to direct to him. I will close with my love to you as a devoted son. Probably I will write some in the morning if Lt.Liddell dont start too soon. So nothing more. Excuse this sorry letter for I am in a hurry.

E.P.Landers to Susan Landers

Farewell for this time. Remember me.

Near Richhmond Va
June 21st 1862
Dear Brother,

I take my pen in hand to drop you a few lines in answer to your kind letter. I can say to you that I am as well as common. I have been back to my company 3 weeks. I'm doing very well now. I hope that when these few lines come to home they will find you and Willis both well. As to nuse, I hant got none of much note to write at this time. It is a very squalling time now. We are close to the Yankees and looking for a fight. Every day I have to stand picket or throw up breastworks nearby. All the time, Yankees throwed bums yesterday in the 8th Ga Regt. and killed 6 and wounded many more. There are some of our pickets hurt every day but there hant been none of my regiment hurt yet but I don't know how soon there will be. We have to stand guard tomorrow morning. Marion, I wish I was in the company with you and Willis but there hant no chance for us to get together now. I received a letter from Father a few days-ago. They was all well as common. I have had a long spell of sickness and had to stay in the hospital 2 months lacking 5 days. I did suffer a heap but by the help of God I am well again and I hope that I will have my health the rest of my time. Marion, I hant got time to write much to you at this time. I want to write to Father today and I will have to drill too. I want to see you very bad. It did surprise me when I heard you wuz going to war but I am in hope that you will have your health. There is a rite smart of sickness here in camp now. I must close. I remain your brother.

W.P.Mason to A.M. Mason and M.Mason

Crew's Farm near Richmond Va
July the 6th 1862
Affectionate Mother,

I am once more permitted to write you a few lines to let you know that I am yet alive and is well but that is more than many of my friends can say and

I know that it is for nothing good that I've done that I am spared but a great Blessing bestowed upon me. But the God of all nations has for some purpose brought me through another engagement unhurt and I feel thankful to say so for while many of my brother solgers were slain on the field. The fight was on the 2nd day. We had been pursuing them hot all day Sunday when in the evening we came up with them which terminated in a hard fight. But our regt. was not engaged in it. We stayed there all night and next morning we started out after them again. We marched all day Monday when in the evening another struggle insued lasting from 5 o'clock till 9 with unmerciful fighting. Our regiment got there just as the battle was over. We stayed on the battlefield that nlght. Our line was formed over many dead and wounded Yankeys. We ate breakfast over all their dead some with their brains out on the ground. After eating we formed a line of battle and started out through the woods on another Yankey drive. We marched till about 12 o'clock when news come to us that General Jackson was before us with 30,000 men after the Yanks. Then we turned our course and in the evening we came up with the Yankeys in line of battle in a noble position with a heavy battery in good range of us. We made an immediate attack and with large forces on both sides. But they having all advantages of the high ground and our men not expecting them so close by, our men was not properly organized for the engagement but we had run on them and we was obliged to fight or retreat. The first command given was to fix bayonets and charge the battery which the gallant men in great heroism did but we had to charge through an open field for about a half mile under the open and well directed fire of a heavy battery well supported with infantry. The grapeshot and bumbs cut our lines down so rapidly our officers found it could not be taken. We was ordered back to reform and tried it again but did not succeed and retired the second time. It is amazing strange how any of us got through to tell the fate of the others for all this time we were under the fire of their cannons with the grapeshot and bumbshells flying round us as thick as a hailstorm. Great destruction on both sides but the number is not yet ascertained. There was several of our regiment killed and a good many wounded but none of our company was killed. D.W.Haney was wounded in the knee. The doctor says that he will lose his leg. Medlock was shocked with the bursting of a bumb in his face injuring his eyes but not hurt bad. All the rest of our company come out safe but there was not more than 20 of our company went into it. Some was sick, some tired down and left behind and some was lost from the regiment and I expect some just slipped out. We did not have narry Commissioned Officer with us. They was all sick and tired down but we done the best we could by ourselves. 2 of our Captains got wounded and one of them mortally. He is now dead. A piece of bumb scalped me on the side of the head making a mark but not breaking the skin. It burnt so I thought I was wounded. Next morning I went over the Battlefield and it was awful to look at the scene of destruction that had been done. The field was lying thick with our Noble Southerners being trampled on..............

Letter to Eli's sister, Adaline, from her husband's brother:

Camp Hatten,Tennessee
July the 14th 1862
Dear Sister,

It is that I drop you a few lines that leaves me well at present hoping this will come safe and find you and little Henry well. Also your mother's folks. I received your letter dated the 9th July yesterday and was glad to hear from you. I regret Brother Moten's death very much as he was the only brother I had left in Gwinnett. He was to have been sent home from Chattanooga but he was carried to Moristown and back to Knoxville before he was sent home. That kept him in camp too long but it was not as I or the Captain pleased about sending him home. I was glad we got the chance to send him home as soon as we did as we could not send him no sooner. I would have went with him if I could but there was no chance for that so I expect he fared badly on the road home though I am as well contented about the treatment and attention he received after he got home as if I had been there though I had rather been with him if I could. Not that I think I could a nursed him any better than you did but you know it is human nature for anybody to be with their folks in their last hours. This you know by your own feelings without me saying anything about it.

Adaline,as for the burial care I suppose you had it fixed to your own notions. I write to let you know I am satisfied with all you have done about it. I merely write this to you so you needt be afraid of me thinking hard of you in any way you have managed the care for I am satisfied with it as it could not be hoped for death is sure and life uncertain so I reckon I am as well composed as the care will admit. You stated that you thought he was in Heaven. That gave me some consolation. Adaline I have nothing of interest to write to you. Times is about as usual here. We get plenty to eat at present. We drill about 3 hours a day. We are in Granger County Tennessee. Corn crops some looks well and some are sorry. It is dry here at this time. Wheat was not very good oats not good either. Give my respects to N.B. Also to your mother, in fact to all inquiring friends. So I must close. Write to me again. Give all the news about the crops. As for war news you get more than I do. Tell Caroline howdy. Give my best respects and wishes to her and accept the same for yourself. Write how you are getting along and if you need any money. So I remain your brother

Thomas Hutchings to R.A. Hutchings

Direct to Camp Hatten, Gleens Regiment in Tennessee in care of Captain Dyer.

Portion of a letter written sometime in July, 1862:

You must make out by yourself but I dont know how you will save your wheat but if there is any chance I want you to save it all. Speak to Mr. Arnold and see if he won't cut it for the wheat or the money. If we ever draw I will send you money to pay him but I don't know when we will draw. The Confederacy owes me $100. besides by $50 bounty that will be due me in August which I will send the most of to you if I ever get it. I want you to write soon and let me know what you have done with John and his steers and wagon and all the nuse that you think I want to hear and especially how your crop looks and how you all hold out to work and how you make out to plowing. If you cant send it in one letter send two for I had rather read a letter from you now than anybody else. Give my best respects and well wishes to N.B. and Moten in your letter for I don't know where to write to them. Tell them to write. Remember my respects to-you all as your Best Friend and well wisher. But poor dependent people are deprived of the enjoyment of the pleasures at home that belongs to an independent people and the cussed invaders still trampling our homes and destroying our friends seeking every way to bring us to entire subjugation. It is enough to raise the passions of all persons that claims the title of independent!

Mamma I understand by W.H. McDaniel that you have been buying more corn. I thought you had nearly enough to make out with and I am afraid the rogues will steal it from you knowing that you are alone though it takes a heap to feed 2 horses. Well I have just taken up a mess of boiled pies and read a letter from D.M. McDanieL and Mr. Garner. They was both well. We have some of the hardest rains here that I ever saw. We just have to take it like young goslings but I reckon that the Yankeys has to take it some too. Give my best respects to all the connections and inquiring friends and tell little William Henry that he is my little boy. W.P. has just come into camp. He is not clear of them pains yet though he is nearly well. All that was able to leave had to give up their bed to the wounded. There is thousands wounded from that battle. The boys is all around me so that I cant write as I would wish, but you must excuse me for you know that I would be glad to interest you all that I could and if I never see you no more keep this sorry letter in remembrance of me. H.C. I can hardly keep from crying of you and Add having to swing the plow but I cant help it. You must be careful with the horses and dont run too close nor too fur from the corn and write how your garden patch looks and if you can I want you to send me a wool hat and some thread and needles and a case to put them in for I have lost mine. Give my love to Sarah and "Little Pole" and to Liz and the children. Mammy you need not send me any clothing for we have drawed a suit of clothes but if I send my money home in time you had better get your winter shoes before they get so high and if you can have me a good strong pair of firm shoes made for me for they are from 8 to 10 dollars a pair. You had better get shet of all your cows only one cow and calf. I want to know if you have ever got my overcoat and wool shirt or not. I sent them in Capt. Reeder's trunk so as I have nothing to write I will bring my letter to a close with my best love to you all as an affectionate son and brother and if I never see you on earth let us endeavor to meet in a world where troubles and trials are all banished away. So remember my last respects is with you requesting you to write soon. So nothing more.

Yours Respectfully,
E.P.Landers to Susan Landers

Portion of a letter written from Camp Flora near Richmond,Va:

July 20th 1862
Dear Mother

It is with pleasure that I answer your kind letter of the 24th of June. I never received it till yesterday. It found me in tolerable good health though it was a long time on the way but as older date as it was it afforded me great pleasure to read it for I had not received a line from you since Liddell came. I am tolerable well today all but a little touch of the back ache but I reckon it is cold. I have nothing new to write. E.M. has come to camp but he looks very feeble. I dont think that he will do much good soon. I hardly know how to answer this letter for circumstances has occurred at home since then but you may tell N.B. as for me coming to see him it is a matter of impossibility. I would be glad to see him but there is no chance. I am truly sorry for him for a man in his fix has no business in the Army. They are discharging,a good many in this part of the army and men that is much stouter than N.B. and if I was in his place

I would try for one although one man has as much to fight for as another but if a man is not able to do a thing he cant do it. We have been in regular camp for two weeks. No fighting has been done round here since the first though from all reports I think there will be the worst fighting in the course of a month that has ever been yet for the advance pickets report that the Yankeys are advancing a little everyday back towards Richmond. They have been heavily reinforced. I think it is their full intention to destroy our Capital. Let it cost what it may but oh the destruction that will be among men before they do it. They are now exchanging prisoners. We have taken a great many in this last conflict. The number is estimated at 11,000 in all of the fights. Orders has come in since I begun my letter to be ready to move in 2 hours. I dont know where we will go to but I dont think that we will go far. If they do I will not go with them. It is thought we will only go out to a better place to camp. I wish I could write you an interesting letter but not being very well and having to hasten through to get ready to leave you must excuse me this time for you know how it is here. I am glad to hear that your crop looks as well as it does for I was afraid that you could not tend it and I know it was through great tribulation that you have done it. Give my entire respects and love to Mr. Thomas Matthews. Return unto him my best thanks and well wishes for his kindness to you in time of special need for a friend in need is a friend in deed. Give my respects to Mr. G.W. Shamblee. Give my love to all the Connections and inquiring friends. N.B., since a reflection on the matter I think you acted in a very generous part in going to the War. You have now shown a good will but my advice to you is to not go back to camp too soon for if the fare is as rough in your part as it is here it is no place for a sick man. You said that you and Moten had to ride on flour barrels coming home but I have saw the wounded hauled off in old 4 horse wagons just throwed in like hogs some with their legs off some with their arms off in terrible conditions. I was sorry to hear that Moten was dead. It made me feel so bad to read Add's few lines that she thought he would get well for her hope was in vain but we know not what minute we'll go the same way for death is certain and life is uncertain. Mamma you said you wished I was there to go to the General Meeting. It woulda been a great pleasure to me but I guess you will have a dull meeting but I hope the result will be great. I can turn back to the past time when I was at my old Native and happy home and think of the many enjoyments that was there. It is a pleasure to think of it yet but it is as you said I fear that I will never have the pleasure of roaming my Native Country again. But I will live in hopes if I do not despair it is not impossible. You spoke in regard to my mare. I want you to do what you think best if you can feed her I would like for you to keep her till I come home or till you hear I am dead then I want you to have her but dont injure yourself to keep her. You said something about sending me some money. I don't want you........

Camp near Richmond Va
July 31st 1862
Dear Mother,

As Mr. Beardin is about to start home I will write you a few lines to let you know that I am well. I hope that this may find you all in good health. I read your letter of the 16th which gives me great pleasure for I had been looking for one so long. As for me, I have none of any interest to write. I merely thought that I would write to answer your letter for I think I will answer your letters even if I cant write nothing but compliments. Times is very still here now. We are in regular camp yet and no prospect for any confusion shortly I dont think. We enjoy ourselves here finely now. But we have to drill a heap, but that is good exercise. When I wrote you last I said we was going to move and so we did but we did not go far. We have a beautiful camp ground and plenty of the best kind of water. I would be glad if we could stay here all summer but there is no telling when we wil] have to leave. Ma you ought to be here to eat Irish Potatoe Pie with me and E.M. and A.W. We can make as nice a chicken pie out of potatoes as you ever saw. We make them in a skillet and put butter and pepper in them and they are good aplenty for an old dirty soldier. but they are very expensive. We give 40 cents a quart for the potatoes and $1.25 a pound for the butter so you know it takes our pocket change fast. But I don't care what things is I must have an extra mess sometimes. But it is a shame how we have to pay for things here. Some people is making a fortune off of us soldiers. A small chicken sells for $1.25 and a grown one $2.00. Little hard apples, 50 cents a dozen, peaches $1.00 a dozen, 3 small onions 50 cts. and other things in proportion so you see I will need a right smart of money. But I am going to send you 50 dollars by Mr. Beardin. I want you to use it just as you think best. I want you to use it for the expressed purpose to benefit you and H.C. and I want you to use it when you need it. I would send you more but I thought that I had better keep about 30 dollars for I might get sick and need it worse than you would. We will draw again before long but I must pay Captain Reeder as he is not here now and I feel under great obligation to Mr. Pemberton for the great kindness to me when I could not help myself. I know that you stand greatly in need of all the money that I could send you but somehow or other I feel like I ought to pay him some more for my promise is out. I would like to redeem it so I think I will pay him a little next time we draw if I can see or hear from him, but he has moved out in the country. Ma I was sorry to hear so much bad news in your letter but don't let it put you out of heart. You said something about my little steers and mare.

I think your plans is very good. You can't keep 2 horses and Kate is getting old and I think it is best to sell her and keep Jane and use her like your own. If you want to get a man to work on halfs and can plow her. If I was you I would not try to raise narry another crop, for you are not able to tend it. You have got enough land for the rent to do you. I have not got time to write much. I must hasten through and write again. Give my love to all the family-every one. Tell N.B. to write. I would write him but I didn't know that Mr. Beardin was going till yesterday evening and we had to drill and he is about to start and I haven't time. Tell him to get off if he can for there is men getting off much stouter than him. Give my thanks and respects to Mr. Thomas Matthews. Give my love to all the connections. I hope that I will not always be sending it in letters. I hope that I will be permitted to come and bring but I don't know when that will be for it appears like the Devil is in the people as big now as it ever was. But none save the one who made the men can control them so we must wait for the time to come if it ever does come. Don't be uneasy about me for the life of a soldier just suits me. But I had rather be at home to get some of them big apples before the door. Dry a heap of fruit for it sells for 5 cents a quart here. So I remain your son as ever. Write soon.

E.P.Landers to Susan Landers

July 1862
To Miss H.C.Landers
        A few lines to you Caroline. I am away off from camp about a half mile in an old outhouse upstairs by myself a studying about old times. I have saw more pleasure today than I have in a week for I am tired being with so many men. A person has to slip off if he ever gets to himself. I was glad to hear what you was all doing well. Now you tell Sarah that I can't come before Sunday after my cider. I can almost taste it and them peaches in the old pasture. We have to pay 90 cts a dozen for little hard things and cant get them at no price since we left Richmond. We have to spend a heap of money here. I give 1 dollar for my supper last night down on the river where we was at work. You requested me to send you a ring to remember me by. I will send it with pleasure if I can get one but us old dirty solgers dont have them in camp and I dont no whether I ever will see Richmond anymore or not. But I will send it the first chance. Give my respects to Miss P.M. and Matt and all the Sweetwater girls. Tell Mr. Mc that W.H. and Rob was well the other day. Tell little William Henry to sell mine and his little steers for he cant break them by himself. For the want of room I must close.

E.P.Landers to H.C.Landers at home

August the 1st 1862
Dear Adaline,

      I drop you a few lines that leaves me well hoping this will find you and Henry well. I have nothing interesting to write you. I received your letter of the 16th and was glad to hear from you. I wrote to you some time ago. You said you wanted to get a tombstone for Moten's grave. I would like for it to be done but I think it will be best to let it alone for a while yet until we can see better what can be done, though you can use your own pleasure about it. I will be satisfied with anything you see proper to do about it but as times is hard and likely to remain so for sometime yet I think it best to let it remain as it is for maybe I may get a change to come home some day or other but I fear not soon. If ever I do get home you say if I get sick come and you will wait on me. I will be glad of that. You wrote that Mr. A.C. Jackson said if I get sick, he will come after me and that he will do it. I will call on him. You wrote like you thought that he would take the advantage of me. If he wants to come for me you need not be afraid of that. I am not afraid to trust myself with him in that case for I know him as well as anybody. You said my watch was gone. I have got it. Moten gave it to me before we started. Write to me again. Give all the news so I must close.
Your truly brother Thomas Hutchins

Camp Lee near Richmond,Va
August 4th 1862
Dear Mother,

      As I have an opportunity to send by hand in great haste I will write you a few lines though you need not to expect much for it is nearly night and we have just come off drill. I am well this evening all but one of my jaws is swelled a little. I have nothing new to write at this time. I received your letter of the 16th of July and that is the only one I have received from you in a long time. I sent you a letter and 50 dollars by Mr. F.M. Beardin. Please let me no if you received it. There was 5 ten dollar bills. We are still at the same place, one of the beautifulest camps and a plenty of the best kind of water but I am afraid that we will not stay here long for they have commenced their fighting again with the Yankee fleet on the James River. Last Thursday night they fired their battery at the fleet for about 2 and a half hours supposing to do great damage. We have all enjoyed ourselfs finely since we have bin permitted to rest. We all appreciate this kind of living as hi as we used to at our own homes. As it is most dark I must hasten through. Tell Moss Billy that R.N.is not well. He has bin reporting sick for about a week but he is not very bad off. W.P.Mason is complaining today. Liz, Pink wants you to send him a good pair of No. 9 shoes by the first one that passes. Ma I want you to send me a pair of No. 9's too if you please for I am nearly barefooted and shoes is so hi here. Well you must all do the best you can and I will do the same. I wish I had time to write a full letter but Mr. Ambrose will start soon in the morning and it is most dark. Please write soon and give me all the nuse. Give my entire respects to all the family and connections and inquiring friends. Mamma I think that I would sell what stock I could spare and rent out my land for you can't farm yourself. So as it is getting dark with my best love and well wishes to you as a son. I will close. Excuse this short letter. I will write again soon so nothing more as I remain your affectionate son as ever.

E.P.Landers to Susan Landers

Portion of a letter written sometime in 1862:
My dear Mother ,

I am now about to close my letter and we have had a bad chance to write now for none of us hardly has got any paper. This is some I got in the Yankey camp and it may be sometime before I get to write to you and maybe that this will be the last letter I will ever have the pleasure of writing to you and in it I send my best love and tender affections to you and all the rest of the family and to all the connections and inquiring friends. Tell Harriet and Dan I wrote them a letter a few days before we left camp. I would like to hear from you. I want you to write soon and direct your letter as follows: To Mr. E.P.Landers, Richmond, Va in care of Capt. Reeder 16 Regt.Ga Vol.Gen. Cobb's Brigade. You must do what you think best with what you have got but I would not keep more than one cow. Sell my mare if you think best. I can't tell you what to do. I know one thing, we have got a heap of hard fighting to do but I.dont want you to be uneasy about me for it will do no good for if it is so to be that I fall on the field it will only be as many others has done under my certain knowledge but God never has made anything that he could not take care of and so let us trust in Him and go on. Let the wicked trust Him as well as the righteous so let us be reconciled to our lot while I remain your affectionate son as ever and your well wishes till Death. Closing with my love to you and all the family requesting you to write soon so nothing more for this time. To his mother,

E.P.Landers to Susan Landers

Portion of letter written in the Fall or Winter of 1862

...their legs taken off. I have just eaten my dinner. I will write again. We had some biscuits and water for dinner. I dont like to stay up here. It is too far from the railroad. We dont get supplies enough. We have to buy nearly as much as we draw. As for salt, we dont get enough to talk about. We have to pay 1 dollar a pint for it. I think if the men can stand such a campaign as the last 3 months has been I think they will come home and live always.

Mamma I have studied no little about your affairs and what would be best and I have concluded that you are where you can see what is needed and that your judgment might be better than my advice but I have thought that it would be best to sell your mare and keep Jane and get some sturdy old man to tend your land on halves but be cautious who you get for a mean man would almost break you up in one crop and I think you had better rent that fresh field next to Mr. Shamblee to sow in wheat and when you sell your mare dont take less than her value for horses is very high. I would not keep many cattle but there is one thing I would keep enough hogs to make plenty of meat for if you dont raise it you will get none for there will be none to sell. If you can get one and think you can feed it I would be glad if you would buy me a small heifer if you can get it at a reasonable price and I will send the money to pay for it. All this is merely my thought on the matter but you do as you think best but if I persuade in that way I would have plenty vegetable patches. You can hire them plowed but you make arrangements to suit yourself. My best desires is with you. I want you all to keep in good heart. Dont let disasters and troubles dishearten you for we both have a promise that the Almighty will be a Husband to the Widow and a Father to the orphans. Such will never fail. I received a letter W.R. sent R.N. that stated that him and N.B. was at Moristown at the Convalescent Camp. W.R. said that it would take close attention to ever raise him. It is surprising how they will keep men in service that is not able to wait on their selves nor never will be. There is conscripts here now that cant double quick 50 yards! Give N.B. my love in your next letter. I would write to him but the fact is I cant get paper and stamps for there is none to be had and when we do find any it is so high. This letter will cost me 25 cts and me endorse it so you may guess how it is. This is a cold rainy evening and nearly all of the men will have to lie out and take it but my little tent will keep it off me. I understand that some honest man has stole Aunt Polly's meat and lard. I think that such men ought to be burnt. Give my love to her and all the family. Tell them the last I heard of John he was at

Leesburg sick. Give my love to all the connections excepted tell Sq Mc that William H was well the other day. Give them my respects. H.C. and R.A. and Liz, I would write to you all but the boys has come in the tent and has pestered me so I cant. Tell little W.H. and Charles that they must keep Mamma plenty of wood this winter. Tell Uncle Ely to write to me if he can hear from E.M. and W.H. Car I could not get arry ring to send to you. Tell W.T. I think he has forgotten his solger boy. Liz if Pink dont get back and that box comes what must I do with Pinks overcoat? Let me know in your next letter so I reckon I had better close with my love to you all. I wish I was with you this evening as I once have been. So I bid you good evening.

E.P.Landers to Susan Landers

Battling against the Northern Crimes
Still oft to thee my heart inclines
Though far away in distant climes
Still oft to thee my heart inclines

Camp Lizzie near Martinsburg, Va
Sept 25th 1862
My Dear Respected Mother,

After a long time of silence I am again permitted to write you a few lines to let you know that my respects still remain with you. I am enjoying good health at this time. That is a great blessing. I have nothing of a cheering nature to write. Since I wrote you last I have had some rough times marching from Richmond. We are about 200 miles from Richmond but I think that we have marched 300 miles to get here! We marched 13 days in succession and have been marching nearly every day since we went over in Maryland to see how their pulse beat. We stayed about 2 weeks with a heavy loss. We gained a great victory at Harper's Ferry. There was 12,000 Yankeys surrendered there without attempting to fight their way out. They tried their dearest to get reinforcements and if we had held back 4 hours longer they woulda reached them. The surrender was made on Monday morning at 8 o'clock. The evening before, General McClellan advanced with a large army to help his friends at the Ferry. We then had to almost double quick about 5 miles to meet them and when we got there our force was too weak to stand our hand with them. Now I can't say no more till I tell you the bad nuse. There was about two thirds of our Brigade killed, wounded, or taken prisoner. We went in the fight with 30 men in our company and lost 18 of them though we can't tell who was killed for it was every man for himself. First they fell back on our right and let the enemy flank us. They come in near taking all of our regiment prisoners. There was one time I thought it impossible for me to escape for I was entirely exhausted with heat and the Yankeys right after us and bullets flying round me like hail stones. I will now give the names of the missing. First Capt. Reeder was wounded and left on the field. E.M. McDaniel, A.W.McDaniel, W.~.Mason, Ben Matthews, J.R. Scott, G.R.Davis, G.W.Flowers, Linsy Smith, Green Hamby, G.W.Jackson, John Long, Luit Martin, Samp Garner, T.M. Gazaway, and John Peden. W.P. was wounded in the beginning of the fight. He was shot and some say he was only overcome with the heat. He is either shot or taken prisoner. We have all reasons to believe that A.W. was killed. Ben Matthews was wounded and left on the field, George Jackson was shot in the leg. That is all that we can account for. We suppose the rest was taken prisoner. I tell you it was warm times with the 16th! I feel perfectly lost since the fight for my mess was all killed and wounded that was along but me. It made me feel awful to think that they was all in the hands of the enemy but I could not redeem them with sympathy for I come very near being with them. I stopped once to give up for I nearly give out but the nearer the Yanks came the worse I was scared so I tried it again. It was about dark and what few of us got away got scattered very bad. I traveled till 10 o'clock in the night to get back down to our old station and I got lost and I found an old outhouse and stayed there till morning when I found the regiment. There was only 75 men left in it, 7 in our company. We lay in line of battle till the next morning and the nuse came that Harper's Ferry had surrendered and all the cheering you never heard! Then we marched all day and all night on Tuesday. We waded the Potomac River about day on Wednesday morning and with our little squad went into another hard fight. We only had 5 men in our company. The fight lasted from daylight till dark and some of the hardest fighting that has been. I never saw the likes of wounded men in my life, but none of our company was lost in that fight. I passed through the Manassas battle ground and I saw hundreds of dead Yanks. They had lay on the field till they was as black as a Negro with their eyes and tongues swelled out of their heads. I tell you it was an awful sight. We lost all of our knapsacks and blankets. Now we have to lie round the fire of nights to keep warm. If I had time, I could write a long time but I must hasten through for it is most time for our inspection. We are expecting another fight everyday.

I received a letter that Mr. Mason wrote to Pink but poor fellow was not here to read it. I also received two letters that was sent to E.M. One of them was from his mother and the other from his spicy [sic]. It made me feel bad to read them. I received one for Ben Matthews. Give my love to Uncle Eli and his family and to Aunt Polly. John Matthews was left at Leesburg sick. John Martin is well.

Wig Mills and John Ford got wounded. Barry Norman got wounded in the thigh. I received a letter from Sally Norman. They was all well. I think if this army don't get some rest soon that the men will all die. We have bin marching all day over the mountains and stop at night and start by day. But I have had good health all the time. Mamma you asked my advice about that money I sent you. I think you had better keep it for yourself notwithstanding your debts are to be paid but there is no telling how times may get and and you will need support. You wanted to know if I needed any clothes. If you can get them I would be glad of a good suit of jeans for we are run about so much we can't keep nothing only what we have on our backs and one good suit would last me nearly all winter. But don't send them without you are certain they will come for I don't expect that I ever will get what you have sent me. I haven't heard from you in nearly a month. Give my love to all the connections and friends. Tell them to not think hard of me for not writing for I have no chance in the world to write or I woulda writ you before now. My mind is so confused I cant write as I would wish to. I hate to send such nuse for I no that it will hurt many feelings, but you must not take it to heart too much for it cant be hoped. We can only hope that the Yanks may treat the ones they captured kindly and they may return yet. You must all do the best you can and write as soon as you can and give me all the nuse. I reckon you had better direct your letter to Richmond for there is no telling where we will be and that is headquarters. I have went through many close places since I wrote you last. Perhaps the next close place I will not come through and if this be the last time you ever hear from me I want you to remember that it was God's will for me to go that way which none can hinder. So with my love to you all I will close. Let me know where to direct letters to N.B. So goodby my good old Mother if I never see you again.

E.P.Landers, your son as ever, to Susan Landers

[Editor's Note: Of the people Eli mentions as having fallen at this battle at South Mountain, all returned to the company except the following, who died in Burkittsville, Md at the U.S.Hospital: W.P. Mason - November 27, 1862; Ben Matthews - September 14, 1862; Green Hamby - September 14, 1862; G.W.Jackson - October 16, 1862; Capt. Nathaniel Reeder - Sept. 24, 1862; A.W. McDaniel was captured.]

Portion of a letter written after the battle of South Mountain:

I heard that he said that I was not in the fight at South Mountain and that I run before I got into it and that I never had been in narry fight and all such tales that would degrade an honorable solger. We know the way to find whether those words is well to rely upon is to ask the officers that has been in command of me all the time and see what they say about it. I think they will all say that I have always been found at my post. The rest of the boys that is home on furlough I think will certify the same. I have always tried to discharge my duty in the service of my country as a solger and for him to talk about me in that way it hurts my feelings very much. He has never been in but one fight but if he don't give me satisfaction when he comes back I think he will be in another one. I intend to have satisfaction either by words or deeds. I reckon I have said enough about that for I think more than I say!

Give my love to all the family and connections. Tell Liz that I sent Pink's coat home merely for spite for some of the boys thought that I could not take care of it and they would get it for nearly nothing and I did not intend they should have it under value. Mamma, you said if I needed any clothes you would send them to me. I dont need anything at present, only a shirt at present. If you have the chance I would be glad if you would send me one. I dont know what to do with my filly. I am afraid maybe she will be spoilt if she aint worked some and I dont want to sell her for I feel in hopes the war will end sometime and then I will need her if I should live. If any person that will take good care of her will take her and plow her, let them have her for her feed or if you can get 200 dollars for her take it. Tell E.M. I want to see him very bad. I reckon he enjoys himself finely. H.C. you must tell little Billy that he is too young. I am setting in my tent writing on my knee and all the boys are asleep. I am on guard tonight. I will have to stay up till 3 o'clock. I must bring my letter to a close. My candle is very dim. I want to write R.A. a few lines so with due respects and memory to you as a son I will close. I wrote Aunt Betsy a letter yesterday. Give my love to all inquiring friends. It is 11 o'clock and the drum has not beat yet.

E.P.Landers to Susan Landers

September 1862
Dear Mother,

I got your letter yesterday which I read in good health and with pleasure to hear that you all was well. Mr. Shamblee was here yesterday. He is now at the 7th Ga Regiment and he will return today and I will send this letter by him. I wrote to you on the 25th and there has nothing new happened since. We have fell back about 20 miles since then. I can't tell anything about the enemy's movements since the Fight of the 17th but we have heard from some of the boys we lost on the 14th but our news is not reliable. Capt. Reeder is wounded in one leg and it is taken off. We have not heard from A.W. or E.M. nor Pink, only that all that was not wounded was sent to Washington. I will send you ten dollars by Mr. Shamblee. We have not drew yet but I thought I had rather you had what I can spare than to keep it. You said something in regards to clothes. Don't send,,them without you have a good chance for there is some things lost on the way. Give my love to all the Connections and Friends. I would write a full letter if I had paper. This blank sheet is acceptable though. Send my love to N.B. for I don't no how to direct to him so excuse this short letter and I will close. I have just now received a letter from Lissy to Pink. This is the 3rd one I have received for him so I can't reply to all of them. So nothing more than I remain your devoted son.

E.P.Landers to Susan Landers

Portion of a letter written from Camp Tom near Winchester, Va Oct 12th 1862 Sunday Morning:

Dear Mother,

It is with pleasure that I write you a few lines to let you know that I am well. I have written you two letters lately, but the mail is so uncertain I don't expect you have got them. I have nothing new to write. At present it is very cool and calm here. There is no fighting around now. We have been in regular camp for two weeks. Some thinks we are going to fix here for the winter and some think we will take another trip into Maryland. But as for my part, I have no idea what we will do and I expect I know as much as any of the privates. I have not heard from our wounded boys, only that all that was able was parolled and sent to Richmond. I don't know who was able and as for those who was taken and not hurt we dont know anything about them, though I suppose they were sent to Washington. G.W.Shamblee was out to tell you I was glad to see you all. I sent you a short letter by him for I did not have time nor paper for I had rather talk than write but I knew you would be looking for one but it was a sorry one when it came. I also sent you ten dollars by him. You can let me know if you got it which no doubt but what you will. The weather is getting cold here for the last few days. In my last letter I said to send me some clothes but I dont know what to say about it for we are drawing some little clothes now but its charged to us very high but it would be better to pay a price for them here than to send some to me and I not to get them and then have to pay for them. It is no trouble to get clothing to Richmond but is is a bad chance to get them from there for there is no railroad in 96 miles of us and you know that it is a bad chance to get what you send. I will have to draw a pair of shoes soon. I will just say to you if you get any good chance to send me anything I will pay the man that brings it for his trouble and it will be very acceptable. But without a good opportunity you had better not send anything and I will try to make out without them though I am like a tarapan, all I have got is on my back and that is dirty as common but I am as well fixed as the most of the boys. I lost my blanket in the fight of the 17th. I lay out on the ground till the other day. I bought me a blanket and a small tent which cost me 5 dollars and Thom Matthews, one of my mess, come in from the hospital with a good blanket and we have done well. My mess has decreased for the last three months. Out of ten, they are all sick, killed or wounded but oh what can it be but kind Providence that I am not hurt. I sometimes look back and feel indebted to thank my God for his goodness to me, to preserve me while so many as worthy as I have fell by my side. I have come through 4 engagements without a scratch but perhaps in the fifth one I may fall in the field, but that is the risk to run. I would be glad if they could settle this affair without any more blood shed for there undoubtedly has ever been more blood shed in this war than has ever been recorded before but it is the opinion of the most of the men that there will be hard fighting yet. Tell old Uncle Eli that I read that letter he sent to A.W. by Cain. It makes me feel bad for letters ,to come in to the boys that is gone. One of our sergeants come in the other day and said that E.M. was shot dead but I hope it is not true though I guess you have heard as much from them as I have. I understand that Captain Reeder, W.T. Mason, Ben Matthews, George Jackson has all had their.........

Camp Lizzie near Winchester Va
October 17th 1862
My Dear Mother,
　　　　　I am favored with the opportunity of answering another letter from you which I received yesterday morning and was glad indeed to hear from you all. I am well this morning but as for nuse I have nothing new more than we are expecting another fight now very soon at Charlestown about 15 miles from here. The Enemy made an attempt to advance yesterday and I suppose they took Charlestown and we had orders last night to cook up rations and be ready to leave at any minute though we did not leave last night. But we are now packed up and ready to start and expecting orders any minute. I dont know which way we will go to meet the Enemy and some thinks we will fall back towards Staunton but it is my opinion that we will meet the Enemy and if we do we will have warm times. Our regiment has not increased very much but for

the last month men have been coming in from the hospital and a good many conscripts has joined us. There is some sickness in camp at this time. There is a good many cases of the smallpox with us but there has not been but 2 cases in our regiment yet though it was reported yesterday that nearly all of the 7th Ga Regt had them. I am afraid that they will ruin our army if they get started.

I wrote you a letter the other day and I have no nuse to write today. I merely write in answer to yours and I felt somewhat interested in one part of your letter though I dont know what to say. That is about your arrangements for another year. I have conversed with S.E. Massey about him and he knows all about him. He says that he will not do no good without an overseer and that you know he will not have that and he says that he will ruin my filly.I think that you had better both come under close obligations of writings and have them witnessed by competent men so that he cant falter from the bargain. Give him no advantage for he will take enough anyhow. I wrote the other day for you to be careful who you got but I suppose times is so that a person cant get just anybody, but he has got too many in the family though he may be better than he is represented. I would let Uncle Eli see to matters ever once in a while and one thing I want you to tell him to be very careful with my filly for I would not have her spoilt in breaking for all he would make. For fear you will not get my last letter I will tell you in this, if I was you I would rent N.B.'s upper field and have it sowed in wheat.

A few words to Uncle Eli, if you please when Mr. Cofer moves in, I want you to notice ever once in a while and see that he dont get too large for his trousers thinking there is no man to prevent him. I have not heard from the boys yet but I suppose all of the wounded was sent to Richmond but you have a better chance to get the nuse than we do for we got no papers here.I feel very much lost since the Fight. I dream about the boys often. Extend my love through the family and receive your own portion. So all keep in good heart and do the best you can. Mamma I have drew me a pair of pants and I have got 2 coats and I think I can make out without any from home without there was some certain way to get them. I was glad to hear that you was making enough corn to do you for that is more than many will do. Ma I dont want you to make yourself so uneasy about me for it will do neither of us any good and by the help of God I will try to take care of myself notwithstanding there is many dangers and trials to undergo. But if it be my lot to never return home let us be reconciled. I was glad to hear from H.D. for I had often wondered where he was though I dont know when I will have the chance to write to him nor N.B. for I dont have the chance to write to anybody but you. But the people must excuse me. I want you to write ever chance for I am always so glad to hear the nuse from my old home. I want to know what has become of N.B.'s horse. Give my love to all the connections and inquiring friends. Tell Harriet and children I have not forgot them. Tell Bill and Nick that they are growing up for such times I am now seeing and to harden themselves for it. Tell Mr. Miner that I have not heard from R.N. slince he went to the hospital. Well Mamma, I cant compose my mind to writing anymore this morning. Its roving with you all and on our affairs here so you must overlook all the mistakes. Remember my love for you as an affectionate son and well wishes. I hope the day will soon come when I can return to you again..

E.P.Landers Your Devoted Son till Death

Camp near Fredericksburg Va
November 26th 1862
Dear Mother,

It is with pleasure that I write you a few lines to let you know that I am in tolerable health with the exception of a bad cold. I earnestly hope that this may find you all well. I received a letter from you a few days before we left Culpepper C.H. I was very glad to hear from you but was sorry that so much of the letter had to be filled out with such bad nuse. I was sorry indeed to hear of dear little Henry's death for I always doted so much on him. I could not keep from shedding tears when I read H.C.'s letter about him, the way he done. No doubt but the poor little fellow was apprised of his death. He seemed to be so sensible of everything. As for nuse I have nothing very interesting since I wrote you last. We have moved from Culpepper C.H. about 45 miles. We have had no fighting yet. The enemy left Culpepper and has concentrated a large force at this place. We are here very close together with the Rapahannock River between us. The Yankey camp is on one hill and us on the other in plain view. We have been looking for them to bumb us everyday. They ordered the people to leave Fredericksburg the 21st by 9 o'clock. It was distressing to see the women and little children leaving their homes and all that they had left behind and taking the muddy road on foot. We could just meet them in droves. It was raining and very cold. Their poor little feet was as red as a doves. The people did not have time to make their escape any other way but the enemy has not fired on the town yet. They are fortifying on both sides. I would not be surprised if we did not spend the winter here. The dog is dead about us going to Savannah.

Howell Cobb has been promoted to Major General and sent to Georgia and his brother Thom Cobb is our Brigade general. Some of the men thinks very hard of him for leaving us. I don't like this place much. It is too poor and no chance to get anything only what we draw and that is hardly enough to make out on. Tell W.W. Miner that I received a letter this morning that he sent to R.N. I broke it open for I had no chance to send it to him for we don't know where he is nor nothing about him. In this letter I found more bad nus that was W.D. Cruse being dead. It surprised me when I heard it. I had just been thinking about him. Last night I drempt that I went in a house to warm up and when I stepped in I thought that W.D., Mother, and Miss P.H.was there. I never was so glad to see anybody. I thought I just laid right hold of them and this morning this letter brought the news of his death. It looks like that destruction is spread abroad in our land. So many of our friends dying and other calamities almost as bad but we need not to expect anything better. I just believe that it is the sin and pride of the people that brought it on and I believe the people will have to bcome more equinoxial [sic] before times ever gets any better and times is not half as bad now as they will be. I don't see any other chance only for us all to suffer for the want of common [?] if the War don't close soon and I see no prospect for that. I have studied a great deal about this. I know your force is weak but I want you to try and use some means to make a support without buying it for you know that it is a bad chance. You said that Mr. Cofer had flew the truck. I was very glad to hear that for I was fearful that he would do no good. I think though you had better try and get somebody to tend your land on halfs or rent it. I think if you can get him that Mr. Thom Wood will suit you as well as anybody. I think as Add has met with such disasters that she had better come back to you as she once was. There is no use in her living to herself. I want you to write as soon as you can and let me know how your crop turned out and if you have got hogs enough to make plenty of meat and how will you get salt to put on it and if you have got good winter shoes. If you hant I want you to get them. Let them cost what they may for you have to be exposed to the weather and I want you to have good shoes for I feel the sting of doing without them. I have not got no shoes yet nor no prospect of getting any. The weather is getting very cold. I tell you we suffer for the want of blankets to sleep under. Some nights we don't sleep hardly a bit on account of being so cold. We just have one blanket to lie on and one to cover with. I want you to send me my overcoat and my wool shirt by the first passing for I dont expect we ever will get them things at Richmond. Let me know if you have got any wheat sowed and how much.

November the 29th

As I did not finish my letter the other day I will try it again. We was called off on picket and I had to quit. We stayed on picket 48 hours down in Fredericksburg. I am not so very well today. My cold seems to get worse. I have got a very bad cough and I am so bad stopped up till I sometimes almost smother. I am fearful that I will be sick. We have a very fair prospect for a snow now soon. I dread it very bad without we was better prepared for it. I dont know what we all will do if we dont get shoes. Tell E.M. that he had better stay at home till he gets perfectly well for we see hard times here. All the boys is thinking very hard of Asa Wright for playing off from the company so long. Tell E.M. to write to me. Since I begun this letter R.N. Miner has come from the hospital. He is well and looks well. Tell N.B. to write. Give him my respects. Give my love to all the connections. Tell Nerv Matthews that I was at their house the other night with my darling little Jane. Give my respects to all inquiring friends. Tell them to not think hard of me for not writing for I dont have much chance. Tell Harriet to remember me in naming her son. Mamma if you can I would be glad if you would send me a pair of sox in my coat for I dont expect I will ever get them at Richmond. Maybe by the time I get them I will have some shoes. I want to know if your potatoes was any account. As I have nothing to write and it is most night and very cold and tomorrow is Sunday anyhow, I will close till tomorrow. Perhaps I will have something more to write.

November 30th 1862
Dear Mother,

Sunday has come. I am yet alive and feel smartly better than I did yesterday but I have nothing new to say. The weather still threatens snow. I would like very much to spend this evening with you. All the time it has been when Sunday was some pleasure to me but it is no more now than any other day. Often I have marched hard all day of a Sunday. I want to know if you ever put the bridle on my filly or not. I am afraid if she is not handled some that she will be spoilt. I have not heard from and W.P. since Aunt Sibby wrote to me. I wrote you and her a letter together. I see no more prospect of a fight today. Both sides seem to be calm but we know not what hour they may begin. It has been reported that the Yankeys are reinforcing at Suffolk. We may go there if that be so. My cough troubles me so I can hardly write. I fear it will seat itself in me but dont be uneasy about me. I will try and take care of myself. Tell E.M. to bring me a dram and some pretty girls respects when he comes! Bring the dram anyhow if he cant bring nothing else! I want to see him very bad. I think we could enjoy ourselves together telling,long yarns. Give my love to all of my associates and to all the family. I would like to write to all if I had the chance but they are all included. I had liked to forget there is a misunderstanding among us. Some thinks that it is old Will and some young Will Cruse that is dead. I want to know which one it is. So I must close with my love to you as a son. So nothing more,,only write soon. Farewell for this time. Remember your son.

E.P.Landers to his Mother Susan Landers at home

Camp near Fredericksburg Va
Dec 10th 1862
Dear Mother,

This morning I will write you a few lines to inform you that I am well and I hope this may find you all well. I have nothing new to write as I have just wrote to you the other day. Mr. G.W. Shamblee come in yesterday evening. We was all very glad to see him. He brought everything through safe. I was glad to get my overcoat for I was needing it very bad. It is worth 50 dollars to me for we need everything we can get to keep us warm for the weather is very cold here now. I have been looking for Mr. Shamblee for some time. I told the boys when he come he would bring me my overcoat with some potatoes in it and when I unfolded it I found my words true! I said I would not take 5 dollars for them. I roasted them last night.

Mamma I am at a loss to know what is best to do about clothes. I have got as much as I need all but pants. I have no pants worth anything and if I dont get to draw some before long I will be without and the quartermaster says that we will not draw anymore clothing money. What we draw from now on will come out of our wages so I will just say to you if you can when E.M. comes back to send me one pair of pants. That is all that I need and as for a waistcoat I have got a short coat that will do for now. I dont know whether there will be anymore clothing come in to draw or not. It looks like a heap of trouble to send me so much but I reckon it is the best I can do but I hope it will not be long till I can be at home so they wont have to be sent to me. I am always glad to hear from you. I have had no chance to talk to Mr. Shamblee for he never come till late and and then went out to a house last night and hant come back yet but your letter was a heap of satisfaction to me but it makes me feel bad to hear of so many of our friends dying. Mr. Shamblee has come back now and is going to start back in a few minutes. I will have to hurry through. You must all excuse me for not writing no more. I did aim to write to you all but you see how it is.

Mamma you said that you had 10 acres of wheat sowed on your place. I want to know if it is all yours and I want to know what you will do with the fresh field. I just want to know all about it. It does me more good to hear the likes of that than anything else. You wanted to know if any of that fortune teller words was true. As for being sick I was not well for a week. That much was true and I have had plenty of money to do me so that much was also true but I put no faith in none of it.

Mammy you said you did not have corn to do you. I expect you had better buy some bread corn now for I dont think that it will be any cheaper. You said that you aimed to save the money you got for my steers for me. I dont want you to do it if you need it. I dont want you to suffer on my account. I will send you 45 dollars by Mr. Shamblee and ten dollars to Aunt Cebell McDaniel. That is what I got for the boys clothes. Tell Liz that I let Pink have 2 dollars a few days before the fight and I sold them sox of Pinks for one dollar. I will take it in that way or she can take her pay out of this money. Mamma, Capt Reeder let me have 13 dollars last winter when I was sick and I hant never paid him back. I want you to pay Mrs. Reeder for me. I think she is the one to pay now. This 5 dollar bill on Hamburg I have saved for a long time to send to you. It looks like money used to. I will keep about 25 dollars for myself for we have to spend a heap for something to eat or suffer but I think I can do till we draw again. Ma if Mr. Mathews will plow her himself, let him work my mare some but I dont want a woman nor boy to fool with her.

Add I would like to reply to your part of the letter but I hant got time but it is as acceptable as if I was to write a week. Give E.M. my best respects. Tell him I want to see him very bad. I don't know what is the reason you did not hear from me for I write every 2 weeks. I want you all to write when you can. Give my love to all the family and connections and to all inquiring friends. You write like you thought the war would stop for 4 months. For God's sake don't flatter yourselves with such trash for when it stops for 4 months it will stop for good. If I only had time I could write with more satisfaction but I am hurried so I don't hardly know what I am writing. Tell E.M. to bring me a dram when he comes. Return my respects to Miss Mary, Matt and Miss Paulina. Miss P.H. has certainly fell out with me or I could hear from her. Mamma I am well pleased with your arrangements for another year, much better than I was with your other. Trade with Cofer. I want you and H.C. if you hant got good winter shoes to get them. Let them cost what they may. I have got them you sent to me. Add I am truly sorry for you. Your lot seems hard so it does but dont be discouraged. Liz, Pink will come home as soon as he gets able. We have not heard from them. We are expecting Lieut Martin and Asa Wright to return soon. Their time is out. Mr. Shamblee can tell you as much as I can write so I will close for this time. Excuse this sorry letter for its a hurried up one. Give my respects to N.B. Tell Harriet I will present little Ely something the first chance. So nothing more only my love to you all.

E.P.Landers to his Mother Susan Landers at home

Undated, but obviously written the latter part of 1862:

Dear Mother,

A few lines to you as I don't know when I will have the chance to write again. I am well today. I hope this will find you all well. You must read E.M.'s letter to get the nuse for I haven't got time to write it to you both. I merely write this because I did not have time to send another one by Mr. Shamblee. I sent you 45 dollars by him. I told you I wanted you to pay Mrs. Reeder 13 dollars for me. I want you to pay her and get a receipt from her in my name. It said in my letter that there was no prospect for a fight here and the next morning the Ball opened and we have had some of the beautifulest fighting that we ever have had! The greatest victory of all the war is this according to the number that was engaged. Cobbs Brigade has done the work at last. It is the first time I have ever been out. I think we will try it again soon and I'll tell you I dread it. Of all the fights I've ever bin in I never had such feelings as I had on Thursday and I hope I never will have again. A good many of our Regiment was wounded that day and several were killed. I want you to write soon. My Dear Mother if I never meet you again and should meet the dead fate of some of my friends I hope to meet you in a world of peace and pleasure. There is so many dangers stares me in the face I feel the need of a strong Protector. I sent you some needles by Mr. Shamblee. I merely sent them for compliments. Give my love to all the Family. Excuse these few lines. I will send it in E.M.'s letter so I will quit.

E.P.Landers to Susan Landers

Portion of a letter written sometime in 1862:

....for what cause I cant tell but I have almost lost hope of ever meeting you on earth again though it is not impossible. There was 32 solgers the other day broke the ice and was baptized and old Preacher staid in the water till be baptized 22 of them. I would like to be at old Sweetwater again. Mamma I sent my overcoat home by Mr. McKerley. I thought I had better send it while I had a chance. I have two others one short and one long and I could not take care of so many in time of action. We drew 2 months wages the other day. We are paid up to the first of March but I will have to keep it for I was nearly out of money for I had spent some on my teeth for they was decaying so fast I thought I had better have them plugged and that cost me 15 dollars so I dont know when I can send you any more for I will need what I have got. I said in my other letter there was some talk of the solgers wages being raised but there is nothing of it. In my last letter to you I said for you to sell my mare. I am still in the notion. I think it best for it will not pay to keep her under the present state of affairs. Mr. Ferrill is just from home and he says that out about Lawrenceville if she is the kind of a nag I represent her to be, you can get from 200 dollars to 250 dollars for her. He said he saw very common looking horses sell out there for 250 dollars. He said that old man Stedman at the Factory is buying up young stock so if you can get some Friend to ride her out there when passing and do what they can for me I will be much obliged to them and will never forget them for so doing. I hate very bad to part with her but I see no prospect of the war breaking and if it was to close I would have nothing to feed her and she is too near grown to do well on pasture all the time. Mamma I think perhaps you had better hire some person to work awhile to fix the ground and plant the crop and get everything started and regulated for it is too rough for you and H.C. to undergo without you was well. Mamma I want you to try your indeaverest [sic] to raise a support at home for I tell you I think after this year those that has to buy their provisions will be compelled to suffer for it will not be for sale for love nor money so I think it will be better to lay out your money to get your crop tended than to save it and have to buy. I may be giving you unsound advice but God knows if I thought so I would not. I want you to try to raise your own meat and bread and if you get nothing else you will not suffer so I will say no more about that. Tell Liz that Capt Cain says that he thinks she can get her money without any trouble. Give my love to all the family. Tell them all to remember their devoted Brother though many miles from them. How gratifying it is to me to take my pen to address you all. I would not take no money for the art of the pen but this may be the last time I may have the pleasure of writing to you and I would be glad if I could be more interesting. I want to know if Brother Tiry expressed his sentiments or feelings about your home if he aimed to have it sold at the appointed time or if he seemed willing for you to still remain at home. Please send me N.B.Landers address. I want to write to him and I have forgotten his company and regiment and station. If E.M. is not gone tell him to come with a stout heart. He need not bring too many clothes with him for he cant take care of them.

Portion of a letter written by Eli's brother, Humphrey Davis, while in a Federal prison, sometime in 1862:

...Wealthy sold the cotton we made year before last just before he wrote her the letter the 10th of this instant. At 25 cts per pound it brought 240 dollars so I hope she can live in these hard times. J.M. Sanders said he heard that E.P.L. was dead as he came out home but Wealthy said your letter said he was well. A sergeant in his company was mighty glad to hear it. I was sorry to hear of W.P.Mason and W.D.Cruse's deaths but the Lords will must be done. I hope the Lord will bless you. Frankly Elizabeth, to hear your troubles I hope they are better off. If the Lord wills, I am to come to see you all when I get free again. If I ever get free anymore some of you may think I have left you but dont ever think so for I cant leave none of you out. Adaline I haint forgot you. J.E. Cruse holds you next to Father. Harriet I would be glad to see you, Dan and the children of yours too. Frankly Adaline I am sorry for your losing your infant but not for it for it is better off. I cant be sorry it being better off. So all of you write to me when you can. Direct your letters to H.D.Landers,Co.G, 3Oth Rgt. Alabama Vols. I remain yours in the Land of Love.

H.D.Landers

Portion of a letter that was undated:

I was dreaming I had the winding sheet over my face and had given up the ghost, and about that time I woke up and found out that the time had not yet come. I could not keep from almost rejoicing for my dream was so plain. It would be a glorious thing if I was prepared to meet such a time. I think of it but there is so many temptations and aggravations here that a person is often led astray. It looks like the solgers get worse. Its almost a Band of Wickedness! You wanted to know if I needed anything. I would like to have a pair of drawers for I have throwed away and lost till I hant got but 1 pair and I would be glad of 2 shirts for I hant got but 1. Please send my shoes by the first one passing. So I must come to a close with my best love and affection to you all. I would write some to all if I had room but you must be included. This is one time I wanted to talk to Mamma. Give my love to Dan and Family. I was glad to hear from them. Tell Aunt Polly, John was well 4 or 5 days ago. I dont know where he is now. Give my love to all them and to all inquiring friends. So let me give you my best love and affection as a son and then I must close. Farewell for this time.

E.P.Landers to his Mother Susan Landers

1863

Fredericksburg Va
Jan 14th 1863
Dear Mother,

I this morning take pleasure in writing you a few lines though it seems like a difficult matter to hear from you. I am well this morning. I really hope this may find you all well. I have nothing new to write this morning but I thought that I would tell you that we had received that box of jeans and clothes that was started when I was at home. It come to the company on the 12th. Some of the clothing was very badly damaged and almost rotten, but none of the individual things was injured. I drawed me another coat out of the box but I have to pay $7.50 for it to make those equal that dont get one. But I had rather pay that for such coats than to draw the government clothes. Pink's things were all sound. I taken them in charge though I dont know what to do with them for I havent got any of my own things. I cant take any if we have to march. I have sold them leggins for 2 dollars. The Regiment is about to draw money and I think then I can pay for them. I will do the best I can with it. Mr. Raborn and Tom Todd is expecting to start home on a furlough in a day or two and if they get off I will send the money by them. The furlough is sent to the General to be signed but they have not reurned though I suppose they will be signed.

Jan 21st 1863
Dear Mother,

I postponed writing this letter on account of hearing from Furloughs. They have come last night and Mr. Todd will start home this morning. I hant got time to write you much. I am well this morning and I hope this will find you well but I fear it will not from the reading of the last letter you said for me to try to come home and see you. Dear Mother nothing in the world would afford me more pleasure than to do so but there is no chance to get off but if you dont improve in health before long I want you to let me know it and if there is any chance in the world to come I will come for I dont think that you will live long without you take better care of yourself and it would most kill me to never see you again. If you dont improve in health and desires me to visit you write a special letter to Capt Cain and one to me at the same time stating the case in it and I think the Captain will do all he can to get me a special leave of absence. Ma you all seem to be very uneasy about me for fear I suffer with cold. I dont want you to think so for when we are at camp and not on picket or other duty we fare very well. We have got good tents and plenty straw to lie on and we lie very comfortable. My pillow feels good and soft to my jaws, that one of Pinks.

I let John Wallis and Thom Matthews take a night with it. They are my bedfellows..........

Portion of a letter written in Fredericksburg, Va:

Feb 9th 1863
Dear Mother,

As I have an opportunity to send by hand I will write you a few lines to inform you that I am well. I hope this will find you well and all the family. I have nothing to write as I just wrote to you the other night though I directed it to Yellow River and I understand that it is suspended on account of smallpox. We have very nice weather now, warm and pleasant though there has been some very cold weather here. John Pedon come in today. I don't know whether he has got arry letter for me or not. His baggage has not come yet. Mamma I would like the best in the world to come to see you as you are getting old and declining in health but there is no chance in the world. Lt. Liddell will bring this letter to you. Some men can come home but all of us cant but I hope the day is not far when we will all be at liberty to come home and stay. I want you to take good care of yourself and try to recruit up for I am very anxious to live to see you one more time but you may outlive me yet for the young must die as well as the old. I would not be surprised if we dont have some very hard fighting before long for the Yankeys has got a new commander and he will want to do something extra. I wrote to you the other night that we was under marching orders but we are still here yet. I suppose it was a false alarm. The smallpox is broke out among us again. W.M. Hunneycutt of our company was sent to the hospital with them. I have been vaccinated the 2nd time and my front teeth was decaying so fast that I had 4 of them plugged with gold. It cost me 15 dollars but I thought maybe it would do me as much good that way as any other. For fear that this will be some mistake I will tell you again I sent Jim Cruse 5 dollars and Liz 2 dollars and you 100 dollars....

February 10th 1863
Dear Mother,

A new morning has come but I have nothing new to write. John Pedons baggage come in last night. He brought me a letter from Sis Francis. She said she

115

had not received a letter from me since July. I wrote on one side of the letter that Todd brought that I want you to send it to her. So I will close.

E.P.Landers

Fredericksburg Va
Feb 25th 1863
Dear Mother,

This morning I will endeavor to answer your letter that I was so glad to receive for it had been a long time since I had heard from you. This will inform you that I am well with the exception of a very bad cold. Mr.Todd got back last Saturday night. He brought everything safe through but my brandy and he drank it up before he got here. Mine and R.N.'s too! But he said he would pay it back the first chance. I was so glad to get my butter that I did not think much about the brandy but he brought 2 bottles of brandy to some of my mess and I got as much of that as done me any good. There is 6 of us and after drinking a half gallon of good old peach brandy we was all rich enough! We had a fine feast for breakfast that morning when Mr. Todd brought John Wallis some sausage meat and me some butter. I tell you it made me think of old times. It did not taste like this old Furkin [sic] butter we get at $2.50 a pound. We have got over half of it yet. My shirt come in a good time for I did not have but one. We have had some awful bad weather here of late. Last Sunday was the coldest day I ever saw. I think the snow is now from one to two feet deep. We have had nothing but snow here lately. I have saw more snow this winter than I ever saw in my life. Ma you said that if I needed anything to send for it but I reckon I can make out with what I have got for we cant carry much on a march and we are ordered away from here as soon as the weather gets so we can travel. A large portion of our army has been sent off but I dont know where they got to. But it is thought that we will go down below Petersburg. They are now expecting a forward movment on Petersburg. I am very willing to leave this place for we have burnt up all the wood around here. We have to burn old field pine bushes or tote our oak wood over a half mile. This part of the country is ruined for all the timber is cut down. Mamma you said that you was afraid that H.C. could not plow Kate. I doubt it myself and if you like him and can get him you had better hire that Mr. Roberts for one month or long as you think best. A good months work at this time would be worth a heap fixing up the ground to plant. If you hire him keep him at the plow all the time for you and that is the main thing and if he is a trusty fellow I want him to plow my little Jane. I want her worked some if there is any chance. H.C. yu said that you was going to ride her.

If you're not afraid to ride her I dont care how much you ride her but be very careful that she dont hurt you. If I was there I could trot her through. I know she is great trouble and expense but I am not ready to take what N.B. did for his horse. You said something about paying your debts. I reckon it is a very good idea but keep enough to answer yourself for you may need it and I dont know when I can send you any more for they have paid us all up to the 1st of January. I dont know when they will pay us agian. I understand that Congress has raised our wages 5 dollars a month. You seem to fear that I am very unesy about affairs at home but I reckon that I trouble myself as little about it as any person could for I feel confident that you will all do the best you can and I know everything must work our accordingly and there is no use to study too much about it. I know you all have hard times but I cant help it. It is hard everywhere but I had rather live on dry bread the rest of my life and live in peace than to remain here exposed to so many exposures and dangers. But I expect to serve as long as the Revolutioners did if I should live unless honorably discharged sooner for I see the evil of deserters. There has 4 or 5 of this brigade deserted and when they brought them back they looked like they was sent for and could not come. They are now under guard waiting for their trial.

Adaline you must take this for an answer to your letter for it is as much to one as another and I have 5 or 6 letters to write as soon as I can. I was very sorry that Bill Smith lost my letter and did not mail it. I thought of it many times. I was surprised when I took it from round the butter and began to read it but it is too late now. The beautiful little damsel is married now. H.C. you said something about a certain long letter but I dont know when that letter will be written for I expect I know as much about some things as you do so I have no more to say.

This is.a nice warm day. I have sot here and written till I am getting cold. Tell A.W.I received his letter last night. I was glad to hear from him. Give him and all the connections my best love and respects. Give Dan and Harriet my love. Kiss little Ely for me. Give my respects to all inquiring friends and especially to Mr. Thomas Matthews. I could write more but I think it is no use. Liz the Captain says your papers is all right and he thinks he can get the money if he can get off to Richmond to file his claims. He says he has written to see if he can have it tended to in Richmond. If not he will have to go himself and it may be a long time but he will tend to it as soon as he can so I will close with my love to you all.

E.P.Landers to Susan Landers

Portion of a letter written in Fredericksburg,Va,:

March 2nd 1863
Dear Mother,
        This evening I will write you a few lines to let you know that I am well at this time hoping this will find you all well. I just wrote to you the other day. Nothing new since that time only I am afraid that we will be put to some trouble to get supplies to our army for a few days now because the railroad bridge has washed away between here and Richmond but they will have it up in a few days. Mamma, I am going to give my overcoat another furlough as it is most summertime. I will send it home by Mr. McKerley. It is so
heavy till I would have to throw it away this summer and while I can sa~e it I think I had better do it. If I should live till next winter I will need it whether in War or peace. I would send you a nice apple in the pocket but I am afraid it would get mashed. They are so soft and mellow. Mamma for fears you will not get my last letter I will say in this one if you can hire a hand at any reasonable price a month or two you had better do it to start your crop for you. Since I begun this letter Mr. McKerley had heard that he will have to walk as far as Hanover which is 40 miles and his wife and child with him. He cant take my coat but I will send it the first chance. Mamma I have studied a heap here of late about my mare and I see no prospect for peace and she is there on your hands, expense and trouble. I hate to part with her mighty bad but I have concluded to sell her if I can get the worth of her to sell her. Dont take less than 150 dollars for her and if you can get more for her do it. She is worth every dime of that money. You can place the money in some good hands or keep it. If you should happen to trade be very careful who you let have the............

Fredericksburg Va
March 17th 1863
Dear Mother,
        I once more seat myself to write you a few lines which will inform you that I am in good health all except the effects of vaccination. I have almost the afflictions of Job from it. I had some kind of braking out and the vaccination has caused inflammation wherever I am broke out. I can hardly get about without difficulty. I hope this will find you all well. I wrote you the other day but I thought I would write again as I thought perhaps I might not have the chance soon again for we are now expecting active service every day. I think when you hear from us again you will hear of a bloody time. The winter is nearly over and

the summer is near. The fighting must begin soon or it is not to begin. It has begun for they are fighting now in hearing of us. There has ben a continual cannonading all day up the river from here but it is several miles off but I am listening every minute for them to call on us for reinforcements. I think from the way the cannons roar it must be a very hard struggle. But dont let this cause you any uneasiness for such things cant be hoped for the fighting must be done. This war is irristible [sic]. It was forced on us by the proud fanatics of the nation. Now we can only resist it with the ball and bayonet and let us do it courageously even if we die in the attempt. Let us implore the mercy of God to be with us in such trying times. Oh that I could reflect more seriously on these things. Could I only forsake so many worldly things and seek the welfare of immortality, the word of truth. So now is the accepted time if I could only view it in that way but it seems like this is not the time for me if I have any time. Oh that I could only see you and converse with you a while. This evening somehow I have had a particular anxiety to see you here lately........

Portion of a letter written from a camp near Fredericksburg,Va.

March 29th 1863
Dear Mother,

       This Sabbath morning I will endeavor to inform you that I am well hoping this will find you all in the best of health. I have nothing new to write at present. E.M. has got back to camp. He is well and seems to enjoy himself finely. I thought that I would wait a chance to converse satisfactorially but it seems like we can never get off together without some of the boys with us. But he has given me great satisfaction but looks like he cant think of much that you told him to tell me. I received your letter and them pants. I have not unrolled them yet. I was glad to hear that you had plenty of provisions to do you this year. E.M. says you have got nice hogs. I want you to try to keep them through the summer. You said you was going to keep my mare and since E.M. has told me how things is I dont care if you do, for money is not much account now. But as you say if you can get 250 dollars for her let her slip. E.M. says he is afraid you all will spoil her being afraid of her. Dont give way to her or you cant do nothing with her. I want her plowed some this summer if there is any chance. I am sorry that you did not get your corn ground broke up for I am afraid that it will be hard to tend. I want you if you and H.C. can't tend your field to hire it done for I tell you it is best to prepare a support at home. Endeavor to raise a good potato patch and garden for they are a great thing. Mamma I have run out of money at last. I only had 30 dollars and I bought me a splendid pair of shoes for 6 dollars and 50 cts. and I bought me a very nice doubled-cased watch. It will cost me about 30 dollars. I thought I had as live have a good watch as to have the money for if I should ever have the luck to be a prisoner it would be worth more than money and I always had to borrow one when I was on guard. But I reckon I can make out without money but it is the first time I have ever been out since I've been in service. Mamma there has some boys come in from the Legion. I will quit and finish this evening. Good by. Maybe I can interest you........

Letter from Eli's brother Napoleon who is in Vicksburg, Miss.
April the 23rd 1863
Dear Cousin,

I take my pen in hand to let you know how I am getting on. I aint well nor hast bin for a week but I hope these lines will come safe to hand and find you all well. I hant got much to write but the Yankees passes with the gunboats every day. When they get ready we will have it with them somewhere. Before long we will leave here soon. I think we will go to Mobile but I dont know where we will go. The health in the army here is bad. The men die here fast if you call eight hundred deaths in Vicksburg a lot. All day they are sent to the hospital. We cant live on what we draw. The meat we draw is spoilt and the beef is so pore we cant eat it. A man cant live here without he spends two dollars a day. I think we will have to gnve it up and come home. Our men look so pore and bad and dont care how the drop feels. The men went to the Brigade wagons to see what they had. Some sell lots [sic] and eggs. They sold um 1 dollar for six, 2 dollars for eggs, one dollar for meat. I was so weak they got there first and got all of them. Tell Mama that I dont feel like I will ever see her face again. There is no chance to come home from here. The men dies right and left in front and rear. I pay out from 1 to 2 dollars a day and then go hungry. I'm not able to run about and hunt it up. I have got one letter since I left home. Tell them to write to me or I wont write to them. I have wrote up half a quire of paper to them and havent got no answer from it. Paper is buyed here when we can get it. Tell Sarah that I think she might write to me. Tell D.Miner I have wrote to him three letters and I want him to rite to me so I must come to a close.

from N.B.Landers to W.M.McDaniel

Portion of a letter written after March 29th,1863:

You said you was about to send me some drawers. I am glad you did not for I have got them of W.D.'s and another good pair. My mind is not composed to writing this morning. You must excuse this sorry letter. H.C. you said you wished I was there to help you mend up the log heaps. Them words pierced me to the heart. It made me think of old times when I have spent so many happy moments in that way roasting eggs but I am afraid that it will be a long time before I steal many more to roast! But I hope er long I will be free again to heap. E.M. talked about you all when he got back. It makes me want to come home worse than ever. I want to see all the little children and see how they look and the people in general. But if I never see none of them again, the warmest blood that runs in my veins is full of memory and love for them. But the longing desire of my heart is to live to see you all again. I have become oppressed in mind somehow here of late but I fear it is through no good somehow. I can't reflect seriously and candid enough upon the great important matter upon which my eternal welfare is based. Oh that I could feel more dependent than I do! I know that self righteousness can never be eternlly accepted. We are commanded to become entirely self denied and I have found it impossible without the help of God to do so. I know that life is uncertain and death is shore a penalty of life or death to follow and should I be numbered with the Cursed, God forbid! I feel that I have strayed far enough if I only knew how to return. Dear Mother if my heart is too hard to yield, pray that I may boldly and successfully lay hold of the tree of life and live that I may spend the remainder of my life different to days past and gone.

The weather is very blustry and windy today. The ground is very wet. We have a heap of rain here. There has been no fighting since I wrote you last. It was a severe Cavalry fight up the river. The bad weather is all that keeps off the fighting. I think our boys all seems confident of success when the blow is finally made. Give my love to all the family connections and friends. I received a letter from Cousin Sallie Norman the other day. They was all well. Don't be uneasy about me but remember I remain your devoted son as ever.

E.P.Landers to Susan Landers at home

H.C., E.M. done what you told him to do to me when he got back and what Add told him, all but kiss me. He would not do that nor would I let him for I had as soon a dog would lick me as a boy to kiss me!

May 1863
Dear Caroline,

      I will write you a few lines but I have nothing gay nor flourishing to write. If I write any nuse it must be of a dismal character. You spoke of your fine meeting and pretty girls and of the beautiful rose vine Car, I would be glad if I could be there to enjoy the pleasant season of spring with my old friends but no such pleasure is for me. H.C. you wanted to know if I thought hard of you for spending my money. I dont call it my money after I send it home. I know that you will not spend it for what you don't need and what you really need that money is to get it with. I wish I was at home today so we could ride out on a visit. I would like to try Jane's~springs. I have not been on a horse since the evening before I left home. G. Davis said that you are a splendid hand at the plow. Be careful and dont let Kate run away. I wish I was there to take your place but I have something else to do. Give my love to our friends.

Your brother, E.P.Landers

Give my respects to Miss P.H. I wrote her last Sunday. Corporal N.A. Smith of our company died April 30th with disease. Write soon and tell Liz and old T to write. I hant got time or paper to write anymore.

E.M. is tolerable well and is off on guard. He cant write today but he sends his entire respects to you all. He cant do much good here. Our Great General Jackson is dead! Our own men shot him through a mistake on Saturday night but I just hope we can find another Jackson!

Camp near Fredericksburg Va
May 8th 1863 (after the battle of Chancellorsville)
My Dear Mother,

      Knowing that you will be uneasy till you here from me I will write to you for you will be sure to hear that I was killed in the fight last Sunday for it was currently reported here that I was. But I write this with my own hand to testify that I am yet in the Land of the Living and all honor and glory be to God for his care over me. We have had some awful times here for the last 10 days. We have been in line of battle all the time marching through the woods, muds, and swamps and some part of the army was fighting all the time. We have lost a many a good solger during the time but the 3rd of May our Brigade got into it heels over head and our regiment lost more men than we ever have in arry fight yet. We had to fight them behind their entrenchments. There was some of our company killed 15 steps from their trench. Our company is nearly ruined. At last count we had lost 3 killed dead on the field and 20 wounded. I will give you the names of some of the wounded: Asa Wright, Frank Plaster, Thom Mathews, James Mathews, Dave Johnson, Dave Rutledge, Jo Rutledge, Bill Wommack, Elbert Daniel, Thom Massey, Jim Raby, Bill Hunneycutt, Thom Weathers, Caut Cofer and others, but not many of them seriously. Bill Wommack has lost his right leg, Thom Massey his left arm, Thom Weathers died the next day and Elbert Daniels was shot through the thigh. I was slightly wounded in the hand but I am still with the company. I stayed in the hospital 2 days to wait on Jim Mathews and Bill Wommack. They was badly wounded. Jim was shot near the kidneys. The ball never come out and he was very feeble when I left him. I understand he died today. Poor fellow said all the time it would kill him. He said that a plain token come to him that if he went into the fight he would get killed. The poor fellow looked very pitiful at me when he got shot and begged me to help him but I had no time to lose. It was everyman for himself for they was falling on my right and left and my disposition inclined to try to return the fire with as much injury as possible. We fought desperately to gain the day but after all our destruction we captured the whole passel of the line that was fighting us. They raised from their trench with a white flag and surrendered to us like lambs. Three cheers for the Army of the Potomac! I must brag although our Brigade suffered worse than any other but my Heart is full of thanks for the great skill that has been manifested among us. During the fight we have defeated the enemy. In every attempt we have completed our designated goal and every point we have slain thousands of their men and there is no use to try to give a correct report of the prisoners though I don't think that 15 thousand will cover the number we taken. Several of their generals and many officers of other ranks were taken too. Our troops all seemed to go into it as cheerful as if they was going to their dinner and not very few stragglers behind. The men would march with their heads up and energy shining on their brow and with such a spirit the victory will always be ours. We have drove old Hooker and his blue coats back over the Dare Mark but thousands of them will never get back. They will moulder on the south side of the River. The Rappahannock River is the Dare Mark with General Lee. They can't stay on this side. The Yankeys when we got them started they just......

Camp near Fredericksburg Va
May 17th 1863
Dear Mother,

       This beautiful Sabbath morning I take great pleasure in answering your very kind letter I read yesterday evening. I was glad to hear from you all. I was glad to here that you was getting along with your work in your little farm. I hope you may be able to cultivate and procure a handsome living at home. I feel confident that you will. I am not digesting well this morning. My bowels has been deranged for sometime with dysentery though I am not a past doing duty. My bowels seems to be tender and sore but I hope there is not much the matter with me. Excuse this bad writing for the pen and paper is both sorry. I am sorry that you have been so uneasy about me for I wrote you the first opportunity after the battle knowing that you would be uneasy till you heard from me. I also wrote to some of my friends requesting them to tell you the news but I hope you have heard from me by this time the good news that I come through safe. I am under Ten Thousand renewed obligations to be thankful for my past fortune. What remains for the future none of us is able to tell. It is useless for me to go on and tell all about the fight for if you read my last letter you can get a small idea of the affairs. It is over with now. The enemy was badly whipped and panic stricken but it was done with great slaughter on both sides. We lost many of our boys. I tell you the old 16th looks quite small since the fight. Our company looks like a platoon. We only have 36 men present in the company. We have plenty of tents and room now that so many were killed and wounded who have left their places vacant. Everytime we form the company it makes me feel bad to see so many vacant places in the ranks and to think where we left some of them lying dead in the woods. The Dreadful Sword of Death has trimmed them from our Ranks........

Portion of letter written sometime in May, 1863 after the battle at Chancellorsville:

...to think that two hours before they was shot what good spirits they seemed to be in not thinking that the last sun had risen on them! Just before we went into the fight, E.N.Payne of our company got a nice coverlid and said that was he was going to keep it till he could see his brother, a wagoner, and he could take care of it for him till winter. Then he would need it but the poor fellow needed it in a few hours for his shroud. I tell you Dear Mother a man has no promise of his life therefore we aught to be preparing to be ready to meet the call at any and all times for everything bears witness to the fact that there is a certain time and doom affixed for one and all. We all need the Countersign to enter the Eternal Campaign above. We have heard from some of our wounded boys and they was doing very well, but Jim Matthews is dead. He died on the 8th and he suffered no little. He was shot near the kidneys with the ball lodging in him. We sent his pocketbook and knife to Lawrenceville by a man in the 24th regiment. As for his hat and clothes I reckon they was throwed a way at the hospital. They was never sent to us. As I aforesaid I aught to be thankful for my past fortune for since the war began there has been 7 of my mess died, killed, or wounded while I am here yet almost untouched. I received a light shot on one of my fingers but it is most well. I suppose I would a bin well in this time but my blood is deranged with impure taxination. It seems like losing one of a Family to lose one out of your mess. I got a small sketch from George Davis who said something about Uncle Ely reporting Add for stealing. When you write, write how it was on a little piece of paper all to itself. Let me know how it was. I only want to know for my own satisfaction.

Portion of letter written after the battle at Chancellorsville:

....I wrote to Mr. Matthews concerning Jim. I waited on him 9 days after the fight till my hand got so I could use a gun. Then I went to the regiment. Jim said that something plainly told him that if he went into a fight that he would get killed. There was several in our regiment that expressed their feelings before they went in and every one got killed. Mamma I am glad you have paid all your debts for now is the time while you have got the money. I received that money you sent to me. I was not looking for it but it was very acceptable for I had to borrow some to help pay for my watch. Then I got 5 dollars from E.M. so me and him both was entirely without and had been for sometime so I will divide with him for he did with me as long as he had a cent. It will get us some paper, stamps, and envelopes. Such things is very scarce and seem to grow less plentiful. Good paper is worth 5 dollars a quire. Everything is extremely high. Our wages will not clear our expenses if we ever buy any little nicknacks, especially them that chaws tobacco. My watch is a good doubled-cased one. It is precisely like the one I kept of Motens awhile that he got from John Miner. You said that Kate was very unruly and that you was going to sell her and keep Jane. I expect if you had Jane broke that she would suit you the best for I think she is of a humble disposition. I am listening to hear of Kate's running away with H.C. George Davis says she is in splendid order. If you sell her be sure that you get the worth of her for she is worth a heap of money. From 6 to 7 hundred dollars is my price on Jane. Now I says daily I feel in good heart that you will make plenty this year if no sickness occurs as I learn that wheat is promising. I want you to save all yours if there is any chance. You had better be looking out for a reaper before it gets ripe. I would pay a good price to get it saved. I wouldnt give a bushel of wheat a day if I could do any better. I dont know what the people will do about their taxes. It will trouble some of them to pay it but this war has brought many troubles on us but let us support it to the last. Let none flinch nor falter but stand steadfast and honorably in defense of our rights and our country will be hard to redeem and let everyone bear a part. If you hear from N.B. let me know it. Write how Mr. Matthews is getting along with his Bottom Land. Give him my entire love and respects. Give my love to all the connections and friends. This is a long letter with little interest but I have nothing to write. Times is very different to what they was this time two weeks ago. The cannons were roaring, the balls flying, the wounded groaning and everything that was terror is now peace. While everything is quiet today may it remain so. Remember me your son. I close with love and gratitude towards you Dear Mother. Farewell.

E.P.Landers to Susan Landers

May 26th 1863
Dear Mother,

This morning I will inform you that I am not very well. I am badly pestered with risings on me. I think they originate from impure vaccination. I am afraid that my health is injured on the account I have been afflicted with sores all this spring. The doctors says it may never get out of my blood. I have not been able for duty for several days nor dont know when I will be. But now dont think that I am sick and be uneasy about me for you have suffered more uneasiness about me now than was necessary. I dont know how such reports as me being killed ever got out. People ought to be more careful in their reports. My hand is not quite well yet. I have written to you twice since the fight and has received no answer to them. I would be glad to hear from you. I have been uneasy about our horses since I heard you was out hunting them. You had better be very careful with them or you may lose them for good. Mamma I would suggest that when you plow your corn the 2nd time that you plant peas in the middle if you can get them for they will be of great value for sale and for stock. The vines for cow food they sell for a dollar a quart here. I am glad to hear that the wheat is promising. Give my love to all the family and connections. I will write you again when I hear from you. I received a letter from H.D. the other day. He was a little sick. He said that N.B. was well and Wealthy and little H.D. was making a crop. Little H.D. does the plowing. R.N. Miner is well. Goodby for this time.

E.P.Landers your Son

Camp near Culpepper Court House Va
June 11th 1863
Dear Mother,

I this morning take pleasure in writing you a few lines which will inform you that I am well as to health but still pestered very bad with risings. I have 7 or 8 on me now which renders me very unhappy when marching. I have nothing new to write. We have had some tolerable hard marching here of late with considerable movement taking place in both armies. Since I wrote you nearly all our army is concentrated at this place. We have had no fighting here only the Cavalry had a very rough time day before yesterday but I suppose it was only a raid the Yankey cavalry made over this side of the river. They are all gone back. As for how near the Yankey forces is I cant tell but the two armies will meet before long at some point. I dont think that we will stay here long. I think the army has only stopped to rest and wait on the movement of the Enemy. E. M. is gone to the hospital. On account of his leg he cant hold out to march. I received 2 letters from his folks since he left for him. One come in last night dated June 4th. I was proud to here from you all. A.W. said you was all well and that R.A. and H.C. was gone to Newnan. How in the world did they ever get off? It surprised me when I heard it. I was glad to hear that you got our horses for I was fearful that some person would steal them for there is so many that wants my mare. Everybody that knows anything about her wants her. Mr. J.W. Shamblee says she is the best filly in that country. A.W. said your corn and wheat looked well I am glad to hear. I hope the cruise of oil and barrel of meal will still hold out as it did in ancient days. I have not heard from you by letter in a long time. I am impatiently waiting to hear from you. I dont know how or what to write to you till I hear from you. I want you to write soon and give me all the nuse one more time before we take another trip into Maryland which we all think is very eminent. We all believe that is where we have started. I dread the trip but I went it once and it is not impossible to do it again. My intention is to go as long as I can. You must not be uneasy about me if you dont hear from me often for if we take the anticipated trip my chance will be bad for writing. Mr. Shamblee will start home tomorrow I reckon. I believe I will send my watch home by him. If I do I want you to lay it away in the chest and let it stay there without some person wants to give dollars for it. Dont let no one be opening it, the inside of it. Camp is a bad place to keep one. They are so apt to get out of fix and there would be no chance to get it fixed. You must all do the best you can and I will do the same. They will not take Mr. Walker as a substitute. John

A.will have to remain in the army. He is very much perplexed at the thought. He is here in our company now. I saw John Mathews the other day. He is well and hearty and sends his respects to you all. He says he hant heard from home in 2 months. He wants to hear from them very bad. R.N. Miner is not well and he has been ailing all the time of this march. It looks like we are going to have rain shortly. The farmers is needing it very bad. Some of the 7th Ga boys got a letter from the 36th Ga Regiment stating that they was cut up badly, naming some of the killed and wounded. I am very anxious to hear a correct report. I fear that N.B.is killed or some of our neighbor boys. I understand that our boys has won a glorious victory at Vicksburg. Excuse this sorry letter for I don't know when I will have the chance to write again and dont be uneasy about me and give my love to all the connections and friends and to my Mother especially.

E.P.Landers

Note written by Eli Landers as he was on his way to and from the battle of Gettysburg:

Here is the names of the towns we have been in since we come back in the U.S. This is the greatest wheat country in the world. I never saw the like!

June 26th - Into Maryland. Went through Williamsport. Crossed the Potomac River.

June 27th - Through Hagerstown, Maryland Middleway PA Greencastle PA J June 28th - Marion PA

Chambersburg PA

June 30th - Passed through Faitville (Fayetteville) PA

July 1st - In the night through Cashtown

July 5th - Passed through Fairfax PA

Through Waterloo PA

Through Lightensburg MD

Back through Hagerstown MD

Chambersburg Pennsylvania
June 28th 1863
Dear Mother,
With a glad heart I will answer your letter I received a few minutes ago.
I was so glad to hear from you all as I had went back in the U.S. We had crossed
into Maryland on the 26th but we only stayed one night in that state. We only
come through one corner of it. We have been marching on Pennsylvania soil 2
days and our division is in the rear of the army. Some of our troops is a long
ways from here. Ahead of us they are near the Capital of this state. We aim to
take it before long. We have had a long hard march since I wrote you last and
some very hot weather. It was very severe on us solgers but for the last 10 days
it has been more pleasant. The solgers is getting more used to it. There's hardly
any sickness or straggling in the army for the last few days but during them hot
days there was hundreds of our boys fainted and fell in the road and many of
them died but I have been able to keep up all the way. We have a large army now
in Pa and it is in good fix and fine spirits. We intend to let the Yankey Nation
feel the sting of the War as our borders has ever since the War began. The
citizens takes it very well. They are almost scared to death but we treat them
very well. Our Officer has pressed in a vast quantity of Government Property
of all kinds and some of the finest horses I ever saw and some of the finest beeves
you ever saw. We draw plenty of good beef now. We intend to press all we can
while we are in the Union. Us solgers treats the people with respects when we
want anything and we offer them our money for it and if they refuse it we just
take it at our own price. R.N.Miner was left on the way somewhere at a hospital.
He was not very sick. I sent my watch home by Mr. Shamblee and I am sorry
that I done so. If I had it now I could turn it in for 100 dollars of our money for
I could sell it for Yankey money then I could get things as cheap here as we ever
could in Georgia. This is a splendid country. Everything is in plenty. The people
has never felt the war in their country till now. The Yankeys is mightly troubled
about this movement of our army. They are calling out the militia in a hurry to
defend the Capital but if they dont mind we will get there before their militia
does. We have only marched 6 miles today. We have stopped to rest and cook
up rations and get the Government Property out at town. We will have some
hard fighting before long. We need not to expect anything else but I hope we

will be successful. Dont be uneasy about me. I will do the best I can for myself. If you dont hear from me in a month don't be uneasy for there will be no chance to send a letter soon but I will let you hear from me as often as I can while we stay in the U.S. We don't get no nuse from Vicksburg. They must be in a box or some of us could hear from them. I was glad to hear how your crop was arranged. l think it is all right..........

Portion of a letter written from Maryland or Pennsylvania:

I sent a set of uniform buttons home by George Walker to go on my coat, 16 big ones and 6 little ones. H.C. you seemed to fear that I would think bad of you for going to Newnan. You was perfectly right in so doing. I am glad you went and as for getting your teeth plugged, it was the best thing you could of done. I received your letter from Newnan. I have saw a heap of pretty Yankey girls but somehow I cant help but hate them. H.C. give my respects to the Sweetwater girls. Tell them that I say the Yankey girls looks mighty well but I love them the best-yet! It is most night and I have 2 days rations to cook so I had better close. Give my love to all the connections and inquiring friends. I may never live to get out of~the U.S. again and if not, remember where and how I left my life. I received a letter from E.M. today. He is at Lynchburg, Va. He is tolerable well. Tell all my friends to not think hard if they dont hear from me soon for there is no chance for writing now. If I could see you all now I could tell you so many things that would interest you but I will close this short letter with my best love to you all. Remember me as your son and brother. I am well. Them risings is most all well. Give my love to Mr. Mathews and Family. Dont be uneasy about me. Take care of yourselves. So nothing more this evening. It is Sunday. I could set here and write all evening but I must quit. Goodby to you all.

E.P. Landers, your loving son and brother as ever

Portions of a letter written from a camp near Culpepper Courthouse, Va. July 31st 1863:

Dear Mother,

I received your letter yesterday evening. I was glad to hear from all. This leaves me well and I hope you may receive it in like manner. I have nothing new to write as I just wrote you the other day and give you all the nuse. But I will write a few lines this morning. You said something about selling Kate for 300 dollars. I cant say what she is worth now as everything has got at such a rate. You get the advice of some of the neighbors about it or use your own judgment about it. I hate for you to sell her for I am afraid you dont want to but it looks like that is......

.....Some deal of that kind but I may never live to need it. You requested me to try to come home. You need not to flatter yourself with the thought of me coming for it is impossible for me to do so. No leave of absence is granted at this time. Samp Garner's father is now in Richmond and Samp cant get off to see him. Oh how glad I would be to roll up to my old sweet home one more time! If I had it I would give 500 dollars to be at home for just 2 months. But it is very uncertain whether I will ever see it again or not but I hope my resolution will hold out to stay till I can come up boldly and not have to be concealed. My mind is so confused.........

Dear Mother,

You spoke of something in your letter that has crossed my mind many times since I left home. That was how I looked through I never said a word. I tell you I was past speaking. I never was so heart stricken before now but God himself knew my feelings when I left the gate and they can never be expressed. H.C. I dont care how much you ride Jane but dont hurt her back. I had almost as soon see her as arry brother~ R.N. came in from the hospital yesterday. He is well now. I got a letter from E.M. the other day. He was well all but his leg.1 I see the artillery has begun to move. I dont expect we will stay here much longer. We are all very uneasy about the Yanks coming down about Atlanta. We are afraid our western army likes to retreat too much! H.C. tell Charles I want to see his little kitten. Liz must get Maryann some paper and let her learn to write. She learns her books so fast. Liz I want to know if there is any chance for you to get what is due Pink. You ought to have it. No one has no better title than you. I was at the 7th Ga yesterday. All the Gwinnett boys is well. John Mathews looks the best I ever saw him. Give my respects to all the connections and friends. I dont know what we will do now all the old men having to leave home. It was bad enough before. The war will be compelled to close before long on some terms. I want to hear straight nuse from the 36th and 42nd. I want to know who is killed that I know and what has become of Bill and John and N.B. if you hear from them. Let me know it. The train is now rolling out and I wish I was on it going home. I would be happy enough! I cant think of anything to write so I will close with my respects to you all.

E.P.Landers, your son, to Susan Landers

Camp near Orange Courthouse, Va
August 10 1863
Sunday Morning
Dear Mother,

I read yours of the 30th a few minutes ago. I was glad to hear from you. All this will inform you that I am well and hearty. I have nothing new to write as I just wrote you the other day. Nothing new has occurred since we are between Culpepper and Fredericksburg. I hear no talk of a fight but I reckon they are fixing for another round somewhere. We dont meet very often here in Va but when we do we have bloody times. We are looking for E.M. to come to camp from the hospital today. Rick is well. I received a letter from John this morning. I was very glad to hear from all of the boys and to hear that W.R. Miner was not killed. We heard that he was killed dead and it looked like I never did hate to hear anything as bad in my life for we was always such cronies and had been together so much and to think he was killed but I hope he is not dead and will get away from the yankees yet but they have got many of our friends in their hands and they are beginning to treat them very bad. I would not be surprised no time to hear of the Black Flag being raised on that account. There is some talk of it but I hope the people will use more humanity in this war than that. I am willing to defend our rights under a Civilized Banner but I am very much opposed to the Black Flag. But if the Yankees raises it first I will fight it but if our men raises it first then I am done. Give all the Vicksburg Boys my best respects. Tell them to keep in heart but I know it is bad to fight under officers without confidence. I wish they had such officers as we have got. I think they would be more successful. General Lee has the confidence of our army. We don't~ doubt his loyalty. I would like to be at Sweetwater today. I guess you will have a fine time as it is Communion Day. I dreamt last night that I was there and Miss P.H. and her mother went home with me and when I got home you was mad with me I thought. It hurt my feelings to think I had worked so hard to get to home and find you mad with me! But there is no chance for me to come home but I hope I will live to come back sometimes. I want to see you all very bad. Give my love to all connections and friends. I have nothing else to write. Excuse this short letter for some of the boys wants my pen.

Your son, E.P.Landers to Susan Landers

Orange Co Va
August 21st 1863
Dear Mother,

I will send you a few lines in E.M.'s letter merely to let you know that I am well this evening hoping this will find you all well. I answered the last letter received from you stating the death of Brother N.B. and has been patiently waiting to answer another. I think there will be one for me when the mail comes in the morning. I hope so at least. I have nothing interesting to write at present. Everything is calm at present. No fighting going on about here right now. I cant tell you anything about the position of the two Armies but our Army is at different points from Fredericksburg to Culpepper which is about 48 miles apart. I suppose that both armies is recruiting, fixing for another fight. We are 20 miles from Fredericksburg but I reckon we will move camp tomorrow 15 miles from here in order to get forage for the horses. I am very willing for we have eat out this part of the country.

General Lee has granted one man out of each regiment a 24 day furlough. I guess that one of our company will get one but it will be one that has never been home. Sam Dyer will get one since one of his company drawed for it and he got it. He is so proud he cant hardly behave himself. Mamma, if he comes I wish you would send me a pair of sox for I hant got none and I dont like to do without and as you are making me a coat dont think that I am a great big man and make it too large. I am no heavier than I was when I left home. If you could get the pattern that Captain Cain's coat was cut by, you could exactly fit me for his coat fits me all round but his pattern may be over in Milton where you cant get it. I dont need no clothing at present. I could draw but the government clothes is so sorry and dear I had rather draw the money and send home than to draw the clothes.

I am sorry to hear the dry weather has cut your crops short. I was in hopes the rain would continue and the crops be good. All military duty is suspended for today. The President has proclaimed this a day of fasting and prayer through the whole Confederacy but I think the most of the boys eats a heap and prays but little. But I believe that we will have to be more obedient than we are before we can expect to be delivered from this state of trouble. We will have to deny our strength and acknowledge the Almighty. A.W., I received your letter one night and never got to more than half read it for it was dark and John Wallis lost it. I hant got time to answer it for it is most night and we have to draw and cook a days rations and fix for moving. We will move in the morning at 5 o'clock. I wish that me and E.M. had holt of that basket of peaches you spoke of. We would save you of some trouble. I've not eaten one peach this year nor a ripe apple. Everything of that kind grows less plentiful in this army. Mamma if your mare is fat she is worth more than 300 dollars the way everything is for it seems like that the Confederate money is not so current and I dont know what is the reason. Give my love to all the family and connections and reserve a good portion for yourself. I will write you a letter when I hear from you. Write when you can and let me know where Dan Miner is going. I wouldn't advise him to come to this company. I have several good reasons for saying so. Nothing more.

E.P.Landers to Susan Landers

August 28th 1863
Dear Caroline,

    I will write you a few lines but I dont know whether we can get all our letters in the envelope or not. It will be full of nothing for we have nothing new to write. I've got a very bad cold this morning after washing yesterday. I washed my clothes and had to go without a shirt till it got dry. I wore the skin off my hands rubbing. I washed 2 shirts, 1 pair of drawers, and 1 pair of pants. I hung them out to dry and some fellow taken one of my shirts off of the bush so I lost the shirt and my labor and had to buy another one.

    I was very surprised to hear of the wedding and match of Mr. Franklin and his bride! It was a circumstance I had never thought of. I wish them all the pleasures of life but I rather doubt it. You spoke about you and Cousin Lou and Sallie making cider. I woulda liked very much to a hoped you for fruit is very scarce indeed about here but we drew some apples yesterday. A man just made a sacrifice of his orchard and give up the fruit to our Brigade and they made a detail to gather them and divide them. There was about 1 dozen to the man and it was a large orchard so you can give a guess what few chance we all have by the time all gets some. But I was in a rich streak the other day but we had to move camp and that broke me up. I was on guard at a house 2 or 3 days where they had plenty of peaches and apples and 3 of the nicest kind of young ladies you had better believe! I enjoyed myself well. The People was as kind as they could be and upon the whole of it I fell in love with one of the old gent's daughters! I think her superior to anything I've found in Virginia. Enough about her without you could see her.

    R.N. is well and sends respects to you all. We are camped in the open field. I tell you the sun comes down very hot on us but we have built a large arbor to shasde under. We get plenty to eat since we've got in regular camp. Our diet is corn bread and beef and sometimes bacon. The boys don't like the cornbread much. It is too hard to cook. Our army is badly scattered from Fredericksburg to Orange C.H. We are about half way between but there is not much chance to forage about through the country after vegetables or refreshments of any kind. The Provo Guards will arrest every man they find from camp without a pass from the General. General McLaws has ordered a market house near our camps and for all citizens to bring all the poultry they can spare to that place, there to be paid a reasonable price for it. Soldiers is not allowed to get anything only from that place but I dont think that will be much advantage.

There is one of the 10th Ga Regiment to be shot to death with musketry tomorrow for deserting his colors in time of battle. It is bad enough to be shot without the name of deserting. Bud Nash has deserted. He has been gone about 1 month. He run out of fights just as long as he could without being courtmartialed so I reckon he thought he would leave for good. But he might a been gone long since for all the good he has ever done. I do reckon I've as little sympathy for a deserter as anybody in the world!

W.Mason got back to his company before the battle of Vicksburg and if he got a furlough give my respects to him and all the others. Tell Ely to write the 7th Ga Regt. It's been reported that G.W.Shamblee has beat old Uncle Dan Martin very bad with a stick. If I was him I would be ashamed of myself. Everybody is talking about it! Give my love to Add and Liz and the children. Tell them to write. Give my respects to all the girls. Tell Miss P.H. I wrote her a letter sometime back as long as from here to the Branch! H.C. this is a sorry letter but I'm not in time for writing this morning. You must excuse it and remember I am your brother as ever.

E.P.Landers to H.C. Landers

Spotsylvania Co Va
August 28 1863
Dear Mother,

I received your letter of the 17th the other evening which found me well and this also leaves me well. I have nothing very interesting to write. I've written to you so often till I've run out of nuse but I will try to say something. Everything is silent at this time. No prospect for an immediate engagement about here. We are enjoying a good long rest which we all very much need. I was very glad to hear from you all but sorry to hear of the death of our Preacher Teat. I was in hopes to hear him preach again but I'm in hopes and verily believe that he is gone home to receive the great reward that is promised the finally faithful which aught to encourage us all to try to become one of that party knowing the time is swiftly rolling on when we will receive that great pension of the Fate of Condemnation. We have Divine services in the regiment every night and I am glad to see the solgers take such great interest in it as they do. We all should appreciate and improve the time and opportunities for no time is promised to us only the present. I understand that John T. Pittard is dead. It makes me feel very bad just to think how many of my old associates is gone and they are all experiencing the realities of Eternity while I am yet on the terms of Time and Probation! What a great blessing we will have preaching tonight in our street. We have a Presbyterian for our Chaplain. I reckon I've said enough in regard to that matter without I could be more interesting.

I was truly glad to hear that H.D. was alive yet. I was afraid he was lost with Vicksburg. You said that you aimed to sell Kate if the Government did not press her in. Dont be uneasy about that for they cant take a horse from a person that they need and they cant take my mare either. Perhaps some person will tell you that. They will take her in thinking they will get her undervalue but dont let no one baffle you in that way for you know there is many that would treat you in that way.

I had to quit writing to go on dress parade and I will not have time to finish any letter tonight. Dear Mother it appears that you are very uneasy about me and would rather you would reconcile yourself about me forever. I have a friend that is able and will stand by me in every hour and article of Tribulation though you may never see me again. I was glad to hear that Dan went to Captain Dyers company for he would not a bin satisfied in this one. I was sorry to hear that Asa Wright had give out coming to see us for I need them very bad but I reckon that Sam Massey and Sam Dyers will come home in a few days if their furlough is approved and they can bring them for me. W.H. McDaniel I suppose is at home after another horse and that he is going to take N.C. and John. I am sorry that any of our horses ever had to serve in the Army. I will close for tonight.

August 28th Friday morning
Dear Mother,

There's nothing new this morning. The weather is quite pleasant here in the daytime but it is beginning to get very cool of a night. I must look around for me a blanket. I promised to send you a rubber cloth but I reckon I cant now for E.M. come in from the hospital and did not have narry one and I give him one of mine. I thought that you had a better chance to protect yourself from the weather than him. I guess whilst I'm thus writing that you are in the fodder field. I wish I was with you but I can wish only. I hope to see the Eagle of Peace stretch forth her wings one day. Dont be discouraged. Give my love to all the family and connections and friends. I will have to close and write some to H.C. This will not do for that long letter you are looking from me. You must excuse it and accept it as a token of love and respect as an affectionate son. Write when you can. I cant hear from you all too often. Nothing more.

E.P.Landers to his Mother

Spotsylvania Co Va
Sept 5th 1863
Dear Mother,

I only have a few moments to write as Lt. Garner is most ready to start but I am happy to inform you that I am well this morning. Nothing interesting to write. We are all enjoying ourselves the best we can, nothing to do only cook and eat and drill and no engagement expected soon. Well Mamma perhaps this will be the best chance there will be to send my clothes by Lt. Garner. He is willing to bring them and the weather is getting cool and I will need them perhaps before there will be any more passing. But now I don't know in what condition you are in about it. You may not have the cloth yet and if you have not, it wont make no difference. I only thought this would be a good chance to get them. I dont particular need the coat now but my pants is most worn out. Dont put yourself to too much trouble to get them ready for I know it is a very busy time with you pulling potatoes. I wish I was there to help you but I see no prospect of anything of that kind. Sam Dyer can tell you all the nuse. I made him promise to go to see you. He started 3 days ago. I guess he is at home this morning happy enough. He was so glad he could hardly behave himself! there is no chance for me to get off since there is so many that never has been home. But maybe my time will come sometime.

Tell little Charles that I sent him a little Yankey spoon by Sam Dyer. I got if off of the Bloody Battlefield of Pennsylvania. Tell him he must not lose it. He must keep it to remember his old Uncle Eli. I wish I had some little thing to send all the children but I've nothing but love. I can almost see the little things. Give my love to all the connections and inquiring friends. Tell R.A. and Liz to write.If I could see Liz I could give her a heap of satisfaction about Pink that I cant write. I saw it in a letter that Marion Mason was dead but your letter never spoke of it. I dont reckon it is true.

Mamma if you have not sold her I dont think I would take 300 dollars for Kate. She is worth more than that the way everything is rated these days. You need not be uneasy about the Government pressing her in. E.M. is well R.N. is well and off on guard round a cornfield and he went off mad for we was just making a peach pie. He was mightly hopped up about our pie and about the time we got it on the fire he had to go off on guard. But that is the way of a solger's life! He never knows when he will be called on and they have to obey but I hope we will gain our Independence and freedom sometime but it looks like that one half of the people is not working for they are working for themselves and the Devil! I was sorry to hear of Dick Turners mill being burnt. The likes of that proves what I've just said. I've not heard from you since the

17th of August. I'm anxious to hear from you all again. My old Gwinnett friends has forgotten me! They have just quit writing. Garner is going to start for home now.

E.P.Landers to his Mother

Camp near Chattanooga Tenn
Sept 24th 1863
Dear Mother,
      Knowing that you are very anxious to hear from me I will write you a few lines which will inform you that I am well this morning. There has been some very hard fighting since our Va army has arrived here but our Brigade has not been in no fight yet more than skirmishing. Our troops has been very successful so far. We have drove the enemy some 8 or 10 miles and cleared them off of Georgia soil killing a great many of them and taking many prisoners but the number has not been ascertained yet but I saw 2200 in one drove! Our Virginia troops fights like tigers up here in the West. They say they are going to show them the lick it is done with but I think the Western boys is all right. They are not as bad whipped as we heard they was. They all seem in good spirits. The Yankeys has fell back to Chattanooga to their entrenchments. They are well fortified and we are in the line of battle both parties near each other. It is thought that if we cant flank their position some way that we will have to charge them out of their works and if we do it will be done with great slaughter on our side. There is no other chance for they have got good cannon and rifle works but I hope there will be some way for our Prosperity. I will say no more about the fight till it is over with if I should live to see the end. I like this part of the country very well but the weather is dry dry. The dust in the roads is shoe mouth deep. When marching the dust rises so thick a person can hardly see his way. I was sadly disappointed not seeing some of you when we got to Atlanta. Most all the boys when they got off the train was meeting their relations and I kept looking among the thousands for some of mine but narry one could I find. But I saw a good many of my old friends which was a great satisfaction to me. I saw Thom Hutchins and S.McDaniel, Haymie Liddell and several others. Dear Mother, I tell you it was a trying case for me to pass so near home and not call but I pondered the matter. I thought sufficiently and thought it was my duty to stick to the company, deny myself, forsake home for the present and cleave to the cause of our bleeding country to drive the oppressors from our soil which threatens our own door.I thought we was badly needed or we would not a been sent for. I knew it would not be much pleasure for me to beat home without leave. I may never see you nor my home again but if I never do I cant help it. I expect to be a man of Honor to our country at the risk of my life. I dont want to be a disgrace to myself nor my relations. It is unknown who will get killed in this fight. It may be me and if I do get killed if there is any chance I want

138

my body taken up and laid in the dust round old Sweetwater and I want a tombstone put at my head with my name and my company and regiment, the day I enlisted and the name and date of all the battles I have ever been in. I have spoke to some of the company to see to this matter if they should live and me not. I reckon what little I've got will pay expenses. This is my request if it is possible. Now dont think I've give up to being killed but you know it is a uncertain thing as we are expecting to be called to attention soon so I will hasten through. I want you to write soon. I have not heard from you since the 17th of August. We had a jolly time coming from Virginia but I hated to leave the old state after doing so much hard service in it and now it seems like we are away from home. I shall always respect old Virgina and her people. Give my love to all the family connections and friends and reserve a good portion for yourself. Mr.McCain will tell you how I was when he saw me. E.M. and R.N. is well. Excuse this short letter for we are in line of battle now and not much time for writing. Dont be uneasy about me. Your affectionate son,
E.P.Landers to his Mother

Sept 24th 1863
Dear Eli,

We are about 20 miles from you this morning. We will come as close to the lines as we dare to and we wish you to come out and see us if you can this evening. If you can't we will stay three or four days until you can come. We will come on the ambulance today. We did not know you was fighting when we started from home. Be sure and come out this evening or night. We are all well. All of your boys is coming this week. I never did want to see any person as bad in my life! I can't go back home without seeing you. We went to Atlanta to see you but you was done gone. I never did hate anything as bad. We left home Monday morning and have been delayed on the way on account of so many soldiers. We are at the station this side of Ringgold. We will start towards you in the ambulance this morning cause the train can't get no further. If I thought we would not get to~see you, I would write more. We will stay sometime to get to see you.

Susan and Caroline Landers to E.P.Landers

Rossville, Ga
Oct 2nd 1863
Dear Mother,

I reckon you will hear that I am very sick and I have been but I am getting better. I got worse all the time after you left. Day before yesterday was a very wet day and I come very near going out. The ground was covered in water. Everything wet and no place to lie down and I got so bad off till they started me to the hospital through the rain and I got as far as Mr. Lemmons. I just felt like I was going to die so I went in and just told them I must stay there They soon fixed my bed and done all they could for me. Next morning I come

on here but in a few days I am going back to the company for I get no better fare here than I did there. Don't be uneasy about me and come back. I was afraid that some of the boys would write that I was very sick but I am a heap better. Most well so don't be uneasy.

E.P.Landers

[Editors Note: Eli Landers died in the hospital at Rome, Georgia on October 27th, 1863.]

Appendix

Fragments of Undated Letters

(1) It is getting dark and I must close. Give my respects to all inquiring friends. This is written on leaves out of an old book but you can tell my writing. With my best love and affection to you as a devoted son. I will close so farewell dear Mother and Family.

E.P.Landers to Susan Landers

(2) We had no idea of moving yesterday but if my blood is spilt it will be spilt in defense of my Great Sunny South for that is what I come for and we will get the trial of it before long. But if I never see you again Mamma, remember that you have a son that has staked his life for the purpose of maintaining a great and peaceable country. So Mamma let this cheer you for I feel it in my heart this morning. Car, Bill Dyer says to ask you if you have got to be a fiddler yet. He says for you to keep it till he comes back. Bill is a very sober boy now. Sam is well and sends his respects to you all. Car I want you and Mamma to do the best you can for I fear that you are done with me. Car I want you and Add and Bets Mamma and Harriet to get together and write a good letter for I love to read them.

E.P.Landers

(3) Save the money for no telling who is good for their debts these days. I was in hopes that this War would soon close but from the reading of the late papers I think we may lay down all hopes of peace and prepare for an Everlasting War. I am afraid that we are a ruined Nation but let us not be disheartened for all things must work out to the Will of God. I am in a great hurry. Give my love to all the family and to A.W. and E.M. Write soon and often. Write all the news. We will move camps tomorrow about two miles to where we can get wood handy to burn. I dont know how long we will stay up here in Virginia but I dont think we will stay long. Dear Mother goodby.

E.P.Landers to Susan Landers

The following letter was written by Humphrey Davis Landers, who survived the war, from his home at Wildwood in Randoloph County, Alabama.

Wildwood, Alabama
April 22, 1906
Dear Sister Harriet and family,

       I will write to you to tell you that I am as well as I could expect for my age. As you know I was seventy five years old the 1st day of last December. I am able to be up and moving around every day but I don't work much. But you know I can't keep house by myself. Dora and Daniel are minding the hotel in Heflin. Eli and Idus are traveling selling clothing. The other children are on farms so I just go around among all of them. They all treat me well enough but I can't be satisfied like I used to be. I had rather be able to live at home. If I live and keep well enough I want to come out to see you all in Lilburn a little while this summer. I want to look all over the old home place and some other places. I want you to write to me and tell me how many of the old folks are living that I used to know and them who live around there. Give my best wishes to all. You must excuse the bad writing as I have not wrote much in 5 years. I left Heflin to here last Friday and will stay down here a while. I am like a stray, going to and fro so excuse me this time. That's all. I am as ever your Brother,

Humphrey D. Landers

Since writing this letter I've been looking at the garden and wheat patch. I am here at Humphrey Jr's. They have a big garden planted with many things in it. Some of it hasn't come up yet. He has some wheat knee high and plenty of fruit, peaches and apples.

Index

Martin, Dan, 135
Martin, Lt. John F., 75, 97
Martin, Richard, 69
Martinsburg, Va., 96
Mason, Willard P., 20, 22,
    33, 61, 64, 72, 75, 77, 85,
    88, 94, 96, 97, 99, 110
Massey, S. E., 102, 136
Massey, Tom W., 123
Massey, W. M., 72
Matthews, Benjamin, 43, 97,
    101
Matthews, Eli J., 28
Matthews, James A., 43,
    123, 124, 125
Matthews, John, 23, 72, 75,
    83, 97, 128
Matthews, Tom, 25, 28, 90,
    101, 115, 117, 123
Matthews, William T., 22,
    28, 92
Mayfield, Dave, 59, 64, 68,
    70
Medlock, Thomas L. D., 86
Michal, Mattison, 47
Mills, George, 23
Mills, John, 33, 98
Miner, R. N., 72, 74, 83, 84,
    94, 103, 104, 128, 129, 131
Miner, William R., 18, 20,

37, 41, 43, 46, 59, 132
Minor, Daniel P., 134
Morgan, W. J., 49
Morristown, Tenn., 95
Muthren (captain), 27

Nash, Elly, 42, 53
Nash, R. M. ("Bud"), 135
Norman, Barry, 98
Norman, Sarah, 48, 98

Odom, Andy, 72
Odom, Henry, 72
Orange Courthouse, Va.,
    132, 133

Payne, E. N., 124
Peal, Tom, 55
Peden, John, 47, 49, 51, 97,
    115
Pemberton, William D., 44,
    45, 48, 49, 50, 52, 61, 62,
    68, 72, 75, 79, 91
Petersburg, Va., 19
Pittard, John T., 136
Plaster, Dan, 31, 34
Plaster, Frank, 123